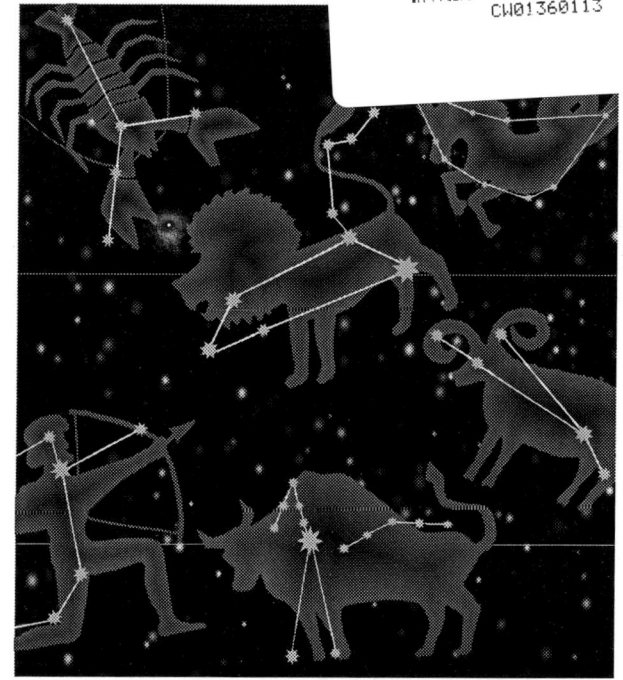

ZODIAC

SOLIHULL

Edited by Lucy Jeacock

First published in Great Britain in 2002 by
YOUNG WRITERS
Remus House,
Coltsfoot Drive,
Peterborough, PE2 9JX
Telephone (01733) 890066

All Rights Reserved

Copyright Contributors 2002

HB ISBN 0 75433 690 5
SB ISBN 0 75433 691 3

Foreword

Young Writers was established in 1991 with the aim of promoting creative writing in children, to make reading and writing poetry fun.

Once again, this year proved to be a tremendous success with over 41,000 entries received nationwide.

The Zodiac competition has shown us the high standard of work and effort that children are capable of today. The competition has given us a vivid insight into the thoughts and experiences of today's younger generation. It is a reflection of the enthusiasm and creativity that teachers have injected into their pupils, and it shines clearly within this anthology.

The task of selecting poems was a difficult one, but nevertheless, an enjoyable experience. We hope you are as pleased with the final selection in *Zodiac Solihull* as we are.

CONTENTS

Arden School

Becci Morton	1
Hannah Kay	2
Nicola Watson	3
Danielle Addison	4
Hayley Wallwork	5
Gemma Truran	6
Heather Starling	7
Esther Matthews	8
Katie-May Joyce	9
Oliver Jacobs	10
Deborah Robinson	11
Jonathan Young	12
Vivian Ajayi	13
Elizabeth Bridge	14
Laura Sadler	15
Philippa Spencer	16
Sam Brown	17
Robert Taberner	18
Stephen Wood	19
Matthew Alderson	20
Rachel Stawarczyk	21
Jack Holloway	22
Emily Hough	23
Bethany Carrington	24
Andrew Clark	25
Matthew Beathe	26
Sarah Guck	27
Harriet Cartwright	28
Alicia Shepherd-Roberts	29
Olivia Jackson	30
Emma Kew	31
Laura Stocks	32
Jennifer Smith	33
Tom Smith	34

Ian Mason	35
Daniel Levene	36
Phil Lewis	37
Olivia James	38
Oliver Marsh	39
Tom Grant	40
Sarah Webb	41
James Walker	42
Amber Hindle	43
Sarah Horsfield	44
Amanda Baynham	45
Philippa Gibb	46
Matthew Gamble	47
Sarah Courbet	48
Gemma Cooper	49
Joe Jinks	50
Lucy Owens	51

Henley-In-Arden High School

Sophie Stevenson	52
Jessica Tunley	53
Thomas Ingram	54
Khato Steer	55
Tim Green	56
Chelsea Thould	57
Claire Whittaker	58
Laura Cherry	59
Elizabeth East	60
Charlie M Higgs	61
Jessica Bonson	62
Jennie Davis	63
George Wishart	64
Thomas Lewis	65
Hannah Davis	66
Amy Clark	67
Nicola Douglas	68
James Roy	69

David Follows	70
Michael Collins	71
Meg Caple	72
Alex Unitt	73
Gillian Grandfield	74
Harry Skelton	75
Ben Shirley-Lobb	76
Ryan Manton	77
Emma Johnson	78
Ben Jennings	79
David Dellenty	80
Felicity Wright	81
Hannah Alexander	82
Emily Styles	83
Hannah Emm	84
Sam Williams	85
Christopher Harold	86
Nicola Guest	88
James Follows	89
Philip Inman	90
Laura Robertson	92

Light Hall School

Chris Smith	93
Charlotte Wakelyn	94
Rebecca Partridge	95
Harry Minton	96
David Alford	97
Lorna Rosie	98
Amy Gardiner	99
Donna Organ	100
Stefan Nowakowski	101
Sophie Priestley	102
Claire Blake	103
Sarah Morgan	104
Harrie Gibson	106

Tom Fleming	107
Charlotte Holywell	108
Rebecca Palmer	109
Charlotte Timmons	110
Emma Gunning	111
Rachael A Chadwick	112
Christine Mackie	113
Lucy Goldingay	114
Gemma Beck	115
Laura Macdonald	116
Sumitra Oliver	117
Rebecca Foster	118
Sophie Chalmers	119
Jennifer Cross	120
Chloe Dale	121
Jonathan Dattani	122
Gregory Day	123
Scott Murray	124
Philip Partridge	125
Charlotte Wright	126
Cally Weeks	127
David Yeomans	128
Charlotte Sewell	129
Megan Timmons	130
Stephanie Perrin	131
Samantha-Ann Medlicott	132
Judith Dray	133
Samuel Drage	134
Lynsey Edensor	135
Jessica Franklin	136
Dale Gilbert	137
Daniel Anthony Hughes	138
Joe Hunt	139
Callum Lyall	140
Alice Hyde	141
Hannah Bluck	142
Chris Carter	143
Chris Cannon	144

Saint Martin's School For Girls

Caroline Hartley	145
Hannah Tildesley	146
Natalie Carr	147
Sarah Curtis	148
Rosie Johnson	149
Laura Hanlon	150
Mary-Anne McEvilly	151
Theodora Manassieva	152
Claire Hall	153
Katherine Morton	154
Nicola Porter-Smith	155
Laura White	156
Hannah Mansfield	157
Rebecca Lewis	158
Sarah Trueman	159
Jessica Banham	160
Rosalind Ievins	161
Holly Harbon	162
Noreen Kumar	163
Sam Greenfield	164
Lucy Archer	165
Kate Pomeroy	166
Katie Morton	167
Rebecca Elliott & Lauren Satterthwaite	168
Gemma Glover & Francesca Williams	169
Melissa Carter & Jaimee Le Resche	170
Bianca Chambers	171
Rosalind Ievins	172
J Banham	173
Kiran Branch	174
Aimee Corbett	175
Katrina Handford	176
Rachel Knowles	177

Solihull School

Michael Horswill	178
Jack Williams	179
Robert Unwin	180
Raymond Cheung	182
Rikesh Chauhan	183
Sam Jackson	184
Stewart Hunter	185
David Diez-Jones	186
James Lishman	187
Matthew Ralph	188
Richard Jerrom	189
Paul Griffin	190
Peter Calvert	191
Tom Harrison	192
Sean Maguire	193
Duncan Brown	194
Oliver Talbot	195
Nicholas Lunn	196
Rob Henderson	197
Anthony Allso	198
David Mundy	199
Brandon Cooney	200
Timothy Freeman	201
Christopher Troth	202
Alistair Higgins	203
Philip Achille	204
Steven Bryce	206

The Poems

I Still Remember

I remember how you used to make me cry,
You used to make me laugh.
I remember how we used to play throughout the day.
I remember you taught me how to plant a seed
and to tie my shoe laces.
You were there when I first walked a few paces.
Then when I was older and a little stronger,
You taught me many more things.
You taught me the things that mattered most,
To cry, to laugh, to love and to forgive.
You taught me many more things and watched me grow.
As I grew, I remember you becoming older and frailer.
Then one awful day you were taken away.
I still remember the way I cried throughout the day and night,
Remember how you held my hand so tight and said,
'Don't forget me or the things I've taught you,
Remember I'll always be there.'
Then I kissed him on the head and said goodbye.
Now two years later I still remember
everything we said and did.

Becci Morton (14)
Arden School

The World

From space, the world is green and blue,
It is as though nothing's wrong, it's as good as new.
But down below it's a different sight,
People run from war in fright -
Bombs are dropped; people die,
And when they have time to look in the sky,
All they see is the sun too strong,
From global warming that will kill the whales' song,
Because the ice caps will melt, the sea will get warmer,
All the food will die, but will get much stormier.
Who made it like this, you may well ask?
Us of course, not a racoon with his blackening mask.
Is it fair that the animals should die,
Or the innocent civilians standing by?
It would be easier to live without all this war,
And terrorism that makes people roar.

Hannah Kay (13)
Arden School

WHEN I WAS SMALL

Who comforted me when I had banged my knee?
Who cooked my tea when I was hungry?
Who held me tight when I had had a fright?
Who took me to the park to fly my kite?
Who hugged me and gave me all her love?
Who called me her little turtledove?

Mum!

Nicola Watson (12)
Arden School

FLOWERS

Red, purple, blue and green
The prettiest flowers you've ever seen
Tall, fresh and smelling sweet
These flowers you cannot beat
Swaying softly in the breeze
Nobody ever dare pick these
And in my garden they do grow
I watch them dancing to and fro.

Danielle Addison (12)
Arden School

SEASONS

The seasons change,
whether good or bad,
spring, summer, autumn, winter,
they're all out there to be had.

The fresh new grass,
so relaxing for my feet,
the cool, soft rain,
that soaks up the heat

The hot sun beats down,
as I lie on the beach,
the cool spring day,
now out of reach.

The leaves turn brown,
it's cool again,
frost on the ground,
days filled with rain.

Winter is here,
snow at last,
snowball fights, fun,
they're such a blast.

The seasons change,
whether good or bad,
spring, summer, autumn, winter,
they're all out to be had.

Hayley Wallwork (13)
Arden School

BIRDS OF PREY

The sky is alive with the sound of birds,
Rooks and falcons flying over in herds.
Swooping down to catch their prey,
Hoping this will be their day.
Talons tense and beaks ajar,
The end of the journey isn't far.
Keeping together like they always should,
Ready now, they approach the wood.

An innocent mouse is shuffling by,
Unaware that it is likely to die.
It carried on normally instead,
The ruthless rooks are overhead.
The sniffing mouse, its food it sees,
The frightening falcons are above the trees.
Swiftly they swoop and with a yelp of pain,
The frail mouse was never seen again.

Gemma Truran (12)
Arden School

FRIENDS AGAIN

Best friends forever, that's what she'd say,
But does it ever stay that way?
For now we've quarrelled and fallen out,
How I wish we could be friends again!

We're both in separate places upset,
How on earth did I ever let
Our friendship turn out this way?
How I wish we could be friends again!

Our friends are trying to make things better
Suggesting that I write a letter.
To apologise for what I've done
So we can be friends again!

I didn't mean to say what I did
About her when she was a little kid.
I didn't know she'd take it the wrong way
I wish we could be friends again!

If thing went back to how they were,
She'd be there for me, I'd be there for her,
Never again would I say things to hurt
If only we were friends again!

Heather Starling (13)
Arden School

LIFE WITH MY NAN

On Monday my nan always came to tea,
She would bring us sweets and sit on the settee,
She always made sure she sat next to me.

Between Monday and Thursday I used to ring her,
To tell her my news and to keep her amused.
She was always pleased to hear my voice,
But would want more often if she had the choice.

On Thursday after school over to Nan's we would pop,
She forgot how to cook so she sent us to the fish and chip shop!

On Saturday mornings she'd arrive in her car,
To spend the day with us she didn't need to come far.
She'd play board games with me, which she loved to win,
When she was losing she always gave in!
Our favourite meal was a roast for tea,
Then we would sit down and watch Jonathan Creek on TV.
It finished at ten so she would go home again!

Esther Matthews (13)
Arden School

THE GRAVEYARD

Creeping through the graveyard,
Middle of the night,
What will I see there?
Will I get a fright?

Creeping through the grave stones,
Icy air,
Tapping on my shoulder,
No one's there.

Creeping past the temple,
Not a sound,
Tripped on a stone,
Heart begins to pound.

Creeping through the undergrowth,
Footsteps behind,
I can hear a breathing,
What will I find?

Katie-May Joyce (13)
Arden School

A Bear

Is that a bear?
A bear up there?
A bear on the stair?
A bear with hair?

Is that a bear?
A bear down there?
A bear down the stair?
A bear on the chair?

Is that a bear?
A bear in there?
A bear in the lair?

Mum! Mum!

Is that a bear that teases?
Oh Mum, not hugs and squeezes.

Oliver Jacobs (13)
Arden School

MUM

You are the sun warming me, filling me with happiness,
You are the rain washing me, taking out my badness,
And you are the lightning warning me away from danger.

You are the thunder telling me when I'm wrong,
You are the wind blowing me in the right direction,
And you are the snow cooling me when I am angry or upset.

Deborah Robinson (13)
Arden School

I'M ALL ALONE

Since you let me go
I thought I was free
I got stabbed in the heart
With a knife of love
That's when I realised
I'd lost you

I find it hard to wake up
When the shades have been shut
You left me there
All alone
With no one to care
I'm all alone.

Jonathan Young (13)
Arden School

Memory

Too scared to turn round in fear that the moment would have passed
Like amnesia, I felt like she had forgotten
And the feeling of love made my cold hands warm again.

Holding on to that second of forgiveness
24 hours felt like a lifetime without her smile
I'll never let go of the glimpse of love that flashed past my eyes
In fear that it'll never return.

Knowing love, once so strong
But now I question its existence
And wonder how it's even possible to lose something
you could never lose, and feel so lost without it.

Day in, day out, from now on and always
I'll hold on to that little time
And hope that the day will come when the feeling of need
will be more than just a memory.

Vivian Ajayi (15)
Arden School

THE SLEEPING BAG!

Whenever I stay at my cousin Mag,
I have to sleep in a sleeping bag.

The bag itself is really small,
And even worse I have to sleep on the floor!

It lives in the attic when I am not there,
And I'm sure maggots rest in its fine, fibre hair.

With its bright green spots and squiggly lines,
It's enough to make anyone with fashion sense whine!

I get in the bag and crank up the zip,
More often than not, I catch my own lip.

It smells of old mothballs, sour yet sweet,
And I'm sure I can smell just a faint trace of meat.

So Aunty and Uncle and sweet cousin Mag,
I really don't like sleeping in your sleeping bag!

Elizabeth Bridge (13)
Arden School

OUT OF TIME!

I looked upon the body,
It was grounded to the bed,
He was now nobody,
Just a figure in my head.

The cleanness of his hair,
I knew that he was mine,
He was always there,
But, I was out of time!

I saw the darkness cover,
The body on the bed,
He was once my lover,
And now he is dead!

Laura Sadler (13)
Arden School

THE INVISIBLE POEM

An invisible poem I thought I'd write,
That's why this poem's out of sight.

Philippa Spencer (11)
Arden School

MY FAMILY

In my family I have a mother
She is nothing like any other
She can be stressful, she can get mad
But otherwise, she's not at all bad

In my family I have a dad
Though he too can get quite mad
If you are careful you will find
That he's really very kind

In my family I've a brother too
If you haven't met him, you haven't got a clue
What he can be like if he gets annoyed
His temper is something you'd do best to avoid

In my family I have a sister
She used to be, well, if you blinked you'd have missed her
But now, she's always hanging about
If you can't hear her moaning, she's probably out!

For now I have told you just of these four
But in my family there are more and more
No, my great big family doesn't stop there
In fact my family is everywhere!

Sam Brown (11)
Arden School

MY DOG

My dog, Gem, barks at the doorbell
    And drives us all mad
When she wants some food to eat
    She looks really sad

My dog, Gem, is a bit of a rascal
    Who bounds wherever she goes
She is as black as the night
    And has a very wet nose

My dog, Gem, has gigantic ears
    A waggy tail and great, big eyes
When you try telling her off
    She looks at you full of surprise.

Robert Taberner (11)
Arden School

MY FAMILY POEM

Whenever I'm unhappy
They are always there
I can always turn to them
Because I know they care.

Of course we have our ups and downs
But there are far more good than bad
I wouldn't change a single thing
They are my family - I love them and I'm glad.

Stephen Wood (11)
Arden School

MY BEDROOM

Up the 'Red Devils'
My room shouts out loud
Walls covered in Man United colours
Of which I'm proud
Sunny room, cosy and bright
Boxers on the floor
I hear the washer woman scream
'No more! No more!'
Football, tennis, trophies galore
Mum and Dad to impress
CD player's on
Blink - rockshow, Papa Roach - infest
The music is loud
'Cause my room's *the best!*

Matthew Alderson (11)
Arden School

STOP IT

Stop it darling, don't do that
Climb on the sofa, or bully the cat
Stop it darling, stop that now
Playing with the knives and wrecking the toy cow
Stop it darling, preferably soon
Answer me back, or bend my best spoon

Stop it darling, stop that love
Pushing me about, do you want a good shove?
Stop it darling, if you could now
Ripping my cloth and starting a row
Stop it darling, stop it honey
Bouncing on the sofa and rattling that money

Stop it darling, soon would be good
Being a nuisance, if you please could.

Rachel Stawarczyk (11)
Arden School

MY FAMILY POEM

My brother is small
I am big
My dad is cool
And my mum is a jewel.

My name is Jack
And I love my sport
I am a dude
And I adore my food.

My mum is called Liz
She is the biz
She loves her books
And she has great looks.

My dad is called Geoff
He is the best
When at the pub he acts like a lad,
But his taste in music is real bad.

My brother is called Tommy
He is real funny
He loves game consoles,
But he hates doing homework.

Jack Holloway (11)
Arden School

My Sister

Her name is Jessica, that's my sister,
In Cockney slang it's skin and blister.
She had blonde hair and bright blue eyes,
And every minute of the day she always cries.
Her big mouth is so wide, it's like a big black hole,
At the end of her nose there's a big brown mole.
She has knobbly knees and wobbly teeth,
She also has a boyfriend his name is Keith.

It's my poor mum I feel sorry for,
Another day with Jess she says she can't take anymore.
Although she's nasty she can be sweet,
Especially when she tickles my feet.
Jessica is not all that bad,
When my mum and dad had her, I was ever so glad.
With her tiny little fingers and her tiny little toes,
With a great big mouth and a mole on her nose!

Emily Hough (11)
Arden School

TIGER

The tiger prowls through the forest mist,
A man spies him and holds up his fist.
You expect to hear a bang from his gun
But he puts it down, behind him is the golden sun.

'I can't do it,' the man said,
He knelt down and put his hands to his head.
Another person came with his knife,
But the man shouted, 'Let the tiger live its life!'

The distant tiger went up to her cub,
Licked it clean and gave it a rub.
The men knew what they were doing wasn't right,
So they backed away until the tiger was out of sight.

Bethany Carrington (11)
Arden School

SCHOOL'S NOT THAT BAD

School is not how your friends say it is like
Teachers don't bite your head off at detention
Or put you on the guillotine when you forget your work
They don't throw you out of the window when you talk in class
Or put you in a pie when you are caught doing rough play

Teachers are actually quite nice when you think about it
They help you with your homework, they give you advice
And help you understand your work,
(But between you and me we all know that teachers
can be a hurricane of anger sometimes!)

Andrew Clark (11)
Arden School

MY HAMSTER

I used to have a hamster
I thought she was very cool
Her name was Maisy,
But she wasn't obedient at all!

At night she used to
Run on her wheel
Then make a squeal
Because she wanted a bedtime meal!

Maisy died on the 22nd of September
She is the one we will always remember
We buried her under the conifer tree
That's where she shall forever be.

Matthew Beathe (11)
Arden School

MY HAMSTER - DASHER

Round and round he goes,
where he is going, nobody knows!

Run, run, run,
I wonder, is he having fun?

Spin, spin, spin,
It looks like he is going to win!

Faster and faster,
Look out, here comes the master.

Sarah Guck (11)
Arden School

MY SISTER

My sister is a real pain,
She always appears to be terribly insane,
I would also mention that she can be terribly vain,
My sister is fifteen years old,
And never seems to do what she is told.

My sister is always picking on me,
During breakfast, lunch and tea,
My sister always thinks she's right,
And she's always the one who starts a fight,
Does she know that she looks a real sight.

My sister thinks she is real cool,
Only you and me know she looks a real fool,
And she always wears real short skirts at school.

But seriously, sisters aren't all that bad,
I think that I would be quite sad,
Without my big sister,
Yes, I'll admit, I would miss her!

Harriet Cartwright (12)
Arden School

The Tiger

With eyes glowing softly in the night,
Shiver and shake, it's a scary sight.
Muscles rippling under furry skin,
All beware of the power within.

Camouflage stripes of orange and black,
Keep to the path and don't look back.
For he's following behind on four huge paws,
All beware of his fearsome claws.

Monstrous teeth like carving knives,
The battle is hard, but he fights to survive.
He prowls around when the sun is low,
All beware who have nowhere to go.

When he roars the vibrations shake the ground,
The jungle stands still at this unearthly sound.
The animals and people flee from him,
All beware for your chances are dim.

Running swiftly across the land,
Paws pound down on the golden sand.
Closing quickly on his kill,
All beware of his powerful will.

Fur that is silky, shiny and sleek,
Beautiful and proud, but definitely not sweet.
A tail that swings from side to side,
All beware he has nothing to hide.

A deadly killing machine that's for sure,
Time stops dead at merely a roar.
A tiger he is and kill he must do,
All beware for he is watching you.

Alicia Shepherd-Roberts (11)
Arden School

PIGZ

Pigs love to wallow in the mud,
They love to snooze and snore,
And they love swill galore.

>Their tales are curly,
>Swirling round and round,
>Their bodies are truly burly,
>And almost touch the ground.

They have round and pinky eyes,
And they love living in stys.
The piglets dash and dart,
Playing their own part.

>Some people say pigs are lazy,
>Some people think pigs are smelly,
>But I think pigs are cool and crazy,
>And I think pigs are lovely.

Olivia Jackson (11)
Arden School

Summer

I love the season summer,
The sand, the sun, the heat,
The fields are full of lush, green grass,
That I feel beneath my feet.

Children play in their gardens,
By the flowers in nice neat rows,
In their little paddling pools,
The little girls' hair all in bows.

I love to go to the beach,
And lay upon the golden sand,
I love to sunbathe in the rays,
In the sea or on the land.

The heats gets so hot,
That I just can't bare it,
All I can do is stop and rest,
And have a sleep for a bit.

Emma Kew (12)
Arden School

PLANTATION DEATH!

It has an old, crumpled forehead,
Dark, grey eyebrows,
Its eyes are deep, dark pits,
It is waiting for bones and blood.

Its crooked nose smells the air,
The sweet scent of the midnight air,
Wondering,
Wondering what is lurking out there.

It has no lips,
Just rows of teeth in its perilous mouth,
Waiting for blood to suck,
Waiting for bones to crunch.

Its face is so huge and manky,
The skin is angry,
Its claws are anxious,
To find something to feed on.

Arms and legs creep onto the victim,
Squish!
Its fangs start to feed from the neck,
The victim is now dead.

Laura Stocks (12)
Arden School

THE CENTOARANO!

Lurking in the shadowy corners,
Eyes flashing like a foxes'.
Bloodshot eyes can be seen through the darkness,
He tiptoes on his hairy paws,
Nails like daggers pierce the ground.
Where there is blood,
A dog is no more.
His mouth is wide open,
Tasting the salty air.
His nose is dripping with blood,
From the maggots up his nose.
His arms feel out where he goes,
But his lair is where nobody knows.
Head the size of a big boulder,
Mouth the size of a melon.
This horrid creature is not good,
To meet in the dark!

Jennifer Smith (12)
Arden School

THE T-REX

A huge, enormous bulbous head,
Eyes, a dark bloodshot red.

Teeth a dark dagger form,
A roar that sounds just like a storm.

A tongue, long, scaly and thick,
Arms as thin as a stick.

Claws, needle sharp right to the tip,
A huge and powerful monster hip.

Skin, all grey, tight like a drum,
Legs that run like a bullet from a gun.

Tail, swinging in the breeze,
Round, powerful with rock solid knees.

Feet that can chase and tear up meat,
Nails that can rip up his meat.

Tom Smith (12)
Arden School

WHAT LIES BENEATH...

Hair as sharp as kitchen knives,
He'll cut you deep within an inch of your lives.
His eyebrows, black and as dark as holes,
His name is Ug and he lives in Knowle.

In his eyes you may see,
A little black world that lies beneath.
The darkness of many sleepless nights,
Shadow his eyes, which show scars from many a fight.

Nose and ears just another ugly part,
Ears are big as a soapbox cart.
He snorts and grunts like there is something up his nose,
Smoke comes out wherever he goes.

The mouth is dingy with teeth as sharp as daggers,
The blood of his prey drips as he stumbles and staggers.
His face is very round, smooth and fat,
Nearly as big as a wild cat.

He lives in a cave miles from all life,
His only weapon ... claws like knives.
He comes out around the town at night,
And if you see him he'll give you a fright.

Ian Mason (13)
Arden School

JUST WATCHING YOU

The monster just watching you,
Just watching,
He's just there!
The horns are like sharp knives,
With a stained kill on the end of them, the stains,
Dried, dripped red blood!
Zebra striped wild wings.
The jet-black eyes looking at you,
Is he behind you?
The sharp, silver fangs just crumble,
Crunch bones!
The tongue is like a wild snake,
Be careful of the bounce.
Be careful of the sharp, silver claws,
He lives in a damp, dark cave,
You hear him jumping, ping-pong, ping-pong.

Daniel Levene (12)
Arden School

JAKE THE RIPPER!

The twisted minded freak,
With his crooked, crumbly, crouched nose,
Just like a hairy beak,
His disgusting, dirty, rotting scalp,
Killing that stinky, sticky, static hair.
His wrinkly, crinkly, decaying ear,
Hidden in his bushy beard of flesh.
His goofy, gory glass ball eyes,
Under his black thorn spots like locust leaches.
His oversized, scary, slashing eyebrow,
Like his sharp jagged, spikes surrounded by the deep,
dark tunnel of death . . .

Phil Lewis (12)
Arden School

PREDATOR OF THE INNOCENT

The creature stares down at its prey from its lofty height,
His cruel eyes wedge onto the scurrying, segmented victim.
As it wriggles through the soft, slippery soil,
The animal arches its feathered, delicate back,
And looks over the many contrasting treetops, his malicious mindset.
A swift swipe of talons and a rush of wings,
As the predator circles its slimy, squirming dinner.
A sharp snatch of claws, a rise and fall of wings
and the deed is done.
The enemy has disappeared, leaving a single sparkling, black feather,
Stained with white, it lies among the crumpled leaves
on the damp ground,
Where the attacker had struck.

Olivia James (12)
Arden School

THE ALLEY MONSTER

The monster has sharp, splintering ears that stand up like a rabbits.
Eyes red and rough glaring at you from the alleyway.
Its pig, square nose with a bullring though it.
A big smile mouth with teeth like knives, to kill and capture prey.
The long arms like metal poles and claws that, with one swipe from
him, you would be merely a few stripes of flesh and bone.
A scaly green body like thick layers of green leather
and a back of splintering knives nicely positioned,
to fire at the prey like a firing cactus.
A dragon's tail to keep its balance when it jumps from alley to alley.
Legs as strong as a concrete brick with a marble coating,
webbed feet like a duck's.
So beware, when you next go into a deep, dark alley,
for you might be walking into a trap!

Oliver Marsh (12)
Arden School

THE MIGHTY OGRE

Huge, hairy horns, sharpened like swords,
Ears like elephants, homed in on any sign of sound.
Eyes, deep, dark, blood struck pits of evil.
Flesh hangs down from his protruding daggers,
Showing the way to his fiery throat of flames.

Mighty arms of steel, a solid chest of gold,
Hands the size of bulldozers, biceps the size of trains,
Feet with blades for toenails,
His cutting claws, capable of carving human carcasses,
Leaving dust so fine it's impossible to see.

Thud! Crash! Bang!
As the ogre moves the crumbling floor cracks beneath his feet,
Houses shatter into minute pieces,
His home, the perilous lair,
Lies, lies waiting for prey, juicy, succulent people.
The mighty ogre rests, until he strikes again.

Tom Grant (12)
Arden School

HARVAMMI

His antennae are tall, troublesome and ready to rip bones
off outrageous, oncoming predators.
While wide, whirling, enquiring, evil eyes are like huge craters
on the moon.

A huge, hugable nose with a very sensitive, sensational,
sense of smell.
With his lovely, large, lanky ears to listen to peaceful people
plotting plans.

Sharp teeth with deep points like shattered rocks under the beautiful
rippling water at the bottom of the river.
His metallic sharp, scorching claws are joined to two, small,
thin, textured, twiggy arms.

His strategic spiky feet clatter as he walks wearily along,
ready to pounce on his prey.
His face may not look scary, but sarcastically he's waiting,
wanting something indulging to eat.

He moves quickly, running, rampaging along like a runaway.
Then he calms and carefully paces, peacefully parading around the
prey.
He stalks slowly but surely, carefully and cautiously, then leaps.

He lives in a small, dark, dingy, closed up, chilled cave.
His home is under tall, beautiful mountains, towering like materialised
mischievous men.

He eats small, interesting, innocent, little creatures.
Then, using his sharp daggers for ripping, crunching and chewing
he has an appetiser and then digs in.

Sarah Webb (12)
Arden School

BUTT UGLY MARTIAN

The Martian, whiskers like a rabbit's
That he's gobbled up.
The snakes on his head hiss and slither.
His devious bloodshot eye looks down
On his fearful prey.
As his slimy tentacles stroll along the boardwalk.
His evil grin, black as night,
Is enough to be an evil sin.
He snorts looking for his food,
Mouth muscles munch, slithering along in a mood.
The places where he lives
Are deep, dark pits of smell.
He eats desserts with his jelly,
In the deep, dark sewers is where the creature lives.

James Walker (12)
Arden School

THE VAMPIRE!

Eyes, as red as blood,
Face, as white as snow,
Teeth, as sharp as broken glass,
Hair, spikes up like razors,
Ears, stick out like an elephant's,
His cloak is a jet-black bat,
He stomps along like an angry giant,
Following you,
    Glaring at you,
        Waiting to,
           Get you!

Amber Hindle (12)
Arden School

THE SPUZZ

Its spikes as sharp as knives,
Its eyes as round as the full moon
And as black as night.
Teeth as jagged as a cliff edge,
It bounces along, springs for legs,
Doing cartwheels like a carriage wheel.
Its home a dim and dreary place of despair.
Its hands clutch a victim and digs its poisonous claws
Into the defenceless creature.
The creature dies a slow, suffering death
As the poison seeps through its body.
It grabs the lifeless body and tears it to pieces.
Its deadly teeth crunching up the bones,
It bounces off, full from its gruesome dinner.
And happy from its victory,
It goes off to find another.

Sarah Horsfield (12)
Arden School

BLOB!

Hair as sharp and spiky as pins and green as grass
His eye is bloodshot ugly and scary
His ears as big as boulders and as floppy as wings
Skin is green and bobbly with slime and scales
His nose so squashed
A mouth like a hole just waiting to get you
Teeth as sharp as kitchen knives
His body so huge just flopped on the floor
Just ready to eat more and more.

Amanda Baynham (12)
Arden School

THE OOGLY BOOGLY

The Oogly Boogly has three throbbing eyes, swivelling in their sockets,
Its ugly nose is pressed as flat as a pancake
against its figure-of-eight face.
Its mouth, a deep, dark tunnel with sharp, sparkling daggers
for crunching the innocent bones of children,
And its spotty skin is so soft and smooth.
On the bottom of its curving body, swirly, slippery, slurping,
sucking suckers suck their way quietly towards its prey.
It lives in your garden, in the bushes or trees that hide it like darkness.
It's waiting to viciously rip you to pieces, to crunch
and munch you for lunch!

Philippa Gibb (12)
Arden School

THE SWAMP SOB

His eyes are deep, dark ditches of doom and despair,
The majestic monster has a green carpet of hair,
The mouth jiggles like jelly with strong, surging blades,
A fireman's hose as a long, bendy nose.

His neck spies over trees and walls,
The creature's arms are short twigs falling from trees,
His hands are like gloomy baseball gloves gripping people's lives,
The legs of the beast are short and stubby like tree trunks,
The claws scratch, slash and scrape with a vengeance,
The brute has warts like the Wicked Witch of the West.

It lives in the shadowy swamps of Florida,
The Swamp Sob waddles along the sombre swamps,
Sobs grind with their teeth and slurp with their tongues,
They eat bugs and drink the bug swarming swamp water.

Matthew Gamble (13)
Arden School

THE MOLERANT!

A hat on his head sits like a crown,
Eyes the shape of leaves are ruby-red like blood.
Ears are orange, glowing and luminous thunderbolts.
Flat and square is his nose.
Little cheeks are pink, but he's not blushing.
Arrow arms, pointing upwards, reaching ready to catch his prey.
His mouth is a large hole of darkness!
Teeth like emeralds glistening.
Claws are spikes ready to pounce.
He swiftly glides across the floor.
He lurks eagerly waiting . . . waiting to catch his prey.
The little mouse scuttles away, safe!
He disappears into the darkness back to his home.
That's the end of him . . .
Till the next time!

Sarah Courbet (12)
Arden School

THE ANONYMOUS ALIEN

You will never know when the alien will land his blood-red sensors,
seeking sounds just waiting for something to come his way.
His three eyes glaring crossed and cracked showing his loss of sleep.
His small, yellow tongue forever sticking out, forever poisonous.
His heart glowing clearly through his orange skin,
an identification for his own planet.
We then come to his claws designed for cutting succulently
into fresh meat.
Be careful wandering around at night, the alien will give you a fright!

Gemma Cooper (12)
Arden School

THE OOBOOO

His hat has dagger-like sticks,
Evil goblin eyes stare as black as night.
Munching knife teeth are as dirty as his torn potato sack clothes.
His leathery skin looks like a snake's skin.
He wears a belt of rats' tails stitched together.
His big knee caps are like rock
She lives in the deep, dark woods in a big, creaky tree
He eats snail soup and fried rats!

Joe Jinks (12)
Arden School

THE MONSTER

The slippery, slimy, squelchy slug has skin like leather
Oozing mucous it slithers along like a snake after its prey
Squashing anything in its way

Its eye is like a whirlpool of hunger
Teeth are sharp enough to cut through steel
Its mouth is like a perilous never-ending tunnel
A fat, flubbery body is slimy and like a ball
This one-eyed monster lives in the dark, depths of my wardrobe
He comes out to eat spiders as they scuttle across the floor
Secretly and silently through the night.

Lucy Owens (12)
Arden School

TIME GOES BY

How many months in a year?
How many weeks in a month?
How many days in a week?
How many hours in a day?
How many seconds in an hour?
Time goes by.

Pisces and Leo,
Capricorn and Virgo,
Cancer and Sagittarius,
Aquarius and Taurus,
Scorpio and Libra,
Gemini and Aries,
Time goes by.

Children grow older,
As do teenagers,
Also adults,
Time goes by.

Horror will pass by,
As will hatrid,
Time goes by.

Time will go by,
But you are you,
You are the best,
Time will go by,
But you will stay throughout time.

Sophie Stevenson (11)
Henley-In-Arden High School

I AM THOUGHTS

I am the things that squiggle around your head
I know all your deepest thoughts and secrets
Who you hate and who you secretly adore
I am there when you need me
The friend you don't need to share with
I am here right now!
I am there when you feel scared or lonely
I am there when you are happy too
When you panic, I help you think clearly
If you need me, I will help you through
In an exam or test, I will tell your brain to get working
Sometimes I jump to conclusions, but nobody's perfect
When you love or hate, I agree with you
And if you need to be brave I will encourage you
I am thoughts!

Jessica Tunley (11)
Henley-In-Arden High School

DEATH

I am Death
I fly through people's hearts like water through a sieve
Giving them the chills
I will not stop for anything
To get you, I will
I wield my scythe with great strength
Slicing everything within my wake
My heart is cold
With breath like ice
I am Death.

Thomas Ingram (11)
Henley-In-Arden High School

I Am Death

I am Death who brings Hell to you
I kill anyone in my way
I take souls from people's hearts
And drain away their prey
I am Death, I am Death
So don't get in my way
Or you'll be in my collection
Stay away, stay away
    Because I am
    Death!

Khato Steer (12)
Henley-In-Arden High School

I'm A Skeleton

I am your skeleton
All white and strong
I keep you from falling
I help you stand up
I keep your brain safe
I keep it intact
I take your punishment
I break and I snap
I keep your heart safe
I keep your lungs breathing
I keep you alive
I am your skeleton.

Tim Green (11)
Henley-In-Arden High School

NEW YORK, NEW YORK!

New York, New York!
The lights have gone out
The air is thinner
The fire is a raging red
The sound of an angry bull
Stampeding to a never land
New York, New York!

New York, New York!
The smell of evil surrounds you
How bitter and cruel it is!
The stench of war is sweating in my blood
The anger fills me up
And my heart is broken
Shattered pieces lie on the floor
The rage and confusion torments me
And I can only dream nightmares
New York, New York!

New York, New York!
Time wails before me
My heart thumping in my breast like a boom box
How painful it is!

The discriminating war is not yet over
I shall stop it!
Goodbye, goodbye sweet New York!

Chelsea Thould (11)
Henley-In-Arden High School

THE GREAT NIGHT RACE

Rushing through the midnight sky,
Fast as lightning, careful not to be left behind,
Running to catch up with the night.

Aquarius leads the way,
Loyal through night and day,
Pisces is next in line,
Very sensitive all the time,
Aries is very confident,
Fast as an arrow that's just been sent,
Taurus lets some others go first,
What good patience that shows,
Gemini is young and witty,
That is why it goes so quickly,
Cancer may be faster than a dove,
But he won't let that stand in the way of love,
Leo is very loving,
To reach his dream he will do by running.
Virgo is so very shy,
So in the shadows she will lie,
Libra is the ninth in this row,
But still can talk you out of any woe,
Scorpio comes after Libra,
Passionate and more forceful than a car,
Sagittarius can be fun,
But joy's his dream and he wants it by the tonne,
Capricorn may be last,
But at least his dreams can also last.

This is the zodiac's great race,
Going on very year.

Claire Whittaker (11)
Henley-In-Arden High School

I Am Scared...

I am scared of everything, the worst of all are ghosts.
They're like sheets that come floating through my window.
When I am lying in my bed
I see them, they sit there staring.
Mum says it's in my head,
but I know they are real.

I am scared of monsters too.
They live under my bed, I wouldn't dare look there.

I eventually get to sleep, but I am woken
once again by those deadly creaks beneath the floorboards.
That's the vampire tiptoeing on my landing.
He never comes in because he is scared of the
garlic on my door handle.

Here I am a prisoner in my own bedroom,
surrounded by bloodsucking demons.
I am so, so scared.
I can't get out because the monsters will get me,
the vampires will bite me and the ghosts will take me away.

Whatever shall I do?
I know, I will wait till morning.

Laura Cherry (11)
Henley-In-Arden High School

I Am Spring!

I am Spring,
I make people sing,
I sweep the land with my flowers,
And wash away Winter's powers,
I make new things grow,
And put on my exciting show,
I'm as happy as children,
And green as the grass,
I watch baby animals being born,
Whose steps are as quiet as ghosts,
I'm magical and calm,
I make people smile,
From every mile,
I make the birds awaken,
And hear them singing,
I am Spring.

Elizabeth East (11)
Henley-In-Arden High School

My Beast

The engine was like a 1,000 horses,
It twisted and turned round the courses.
Its eyes were like two suns beaming down on me,
The engine was buzzing like a bee,
The power behind this beast was great,
This creature is something no one could hate,
As I sat inside this fantasy,
I felt we were flying too high for me,
This thing had so much luxury,
I couldn't believe it was owned by me.

Charlie M Higgs (12)
Henley-In-Arden High School

WHAT IF?

What would it be like if . . .
Clouds were made from candyfloss,
And street lamps were made from liquorice,
    And the sun was made from a great, big,
        chocolate coin . . . glinting like gold?

What would it be like if . . .
    Cats had nine tails and no head,
        And all the year the leaves on the
trees changed to all the colours of the rainbow
        instead of just red and brown,
And if people had no arms or legs and had to
        move along on their tummies?

What would it be like if . . .
Teachers were blobs and couldn't speak or move,
And school was taught on TV,
And homework was to eat sweets?

    Imagine that!

Jessica Bonson (11)
Henley-In-Arden High School

The Monster

Its eyes are as red as the rising sun,
Its claws, like rusty steel,
Its scales are as brown as dirty mud,
Little children, its favourite meal!

It has a tail as pointy as spears,
Its hearing is as sharp as a blade,
The sound of soft snoring it likes to hear,
While its evening meal is made.

Jennie Davis (11)
Henley-In-Arden High School

SKATEBOARDING

S   liding down poles
K   ickflipping through the air
A   iring off a ramp
T   iming your landing
E   xciting tricks
B   ruises and cuts
O   llieing up curbs
A   lways looking for something to skate
R   iding down the pavement
D   reaming of being a pro.

George Wishart (11)
Henley-In-Arden High School

THE SOMME, 1916

On that hot summer's day on July the 1st,
The Brits in the trenches were ordered to stand to,
The officer said,
'The barrage will have killed the Germans,
And the few left will surrender to you.'
The men were ordered to go over the top,
And walk across no-man's-land in a straight line,
And they were told, 'Casualties no more than five percent,
And of course, you all will be fine.'
But on that day 60,000 were laid to rest,
And they went to be soldiers in the army of the Lord.

Thomas Lewis (12)
Henley-In-Arden High School

IMAGINE THAT

Children are aliens,
They eat through their ears.
They are green and slimy,
They have mud as tears.

Some are tall,
Some are short,
They all are ugly,
Just like I thought.

They fly around in saucepans
Up in the sky,
Mind you it must be cool,
Being able to fly.

Some are fat,
Some are thin,
Some have noses,
On their chin.

Some have dogs,
Some have cats,
They are all as ugly as each other,
Imagine that!

Hannah Davis (11)
Henley-In-Arden High School

The Witch

Her shoes so tiny, a mouse could only just fit in them
And her socks as black as coal from dirt.
The feet are as yellow as the sun, with fungi, and are decorated
with warts.
Her nails, which are never cut, are as brown as mud.

A short, thin leg as scaly as a lizard's back.
With knees that are as thin as an ostrich's leg,
And the thighs are as thin as a heel on a stiletto.

Moving to the stomach which is like the thinnest ruler in the world.
Her back always hunched up, maybe it's a hunchback!
Her shoulders that press into her neck make her look like an alien
And her arms as long as a giraffe's neck
With her hands as sharp and scrawny as a bird's claw.

Then comes the head, her gormless face is as ugly as a hippopotamus.
Her lips are as tight as a knot, which can never be undone
And a tiny nose smaller than a budgie's beak.
Her eyes are tiny slits, smaller than a human pupil
And the hair as black as night,
This tops off an average witch.

Amy Clark (11)
Henley-In-Arden High School

WIND

An invisible bird fluttering past,
Moving along, never stops,
Pushing the boulders in the sky,
Squeezing out the black clothes.

Running past its rustling whistle,
Sends waves of green along the Earth,
A broom swipes past, up swirls dirt
A roundabout of colour.

Makes its music in a band,
Marching down the road.
Helping wash maids, drying rags,
That hang upon a string.

It's any colour you want it to be.
Clutching onto your kites,
Pushing boats along the blue,
It's got an endless list of jobs to do . . .

Nicola Douglas (11)
Henley-In-Arden High School

THE SPEEDY BEAST

I saw the Speedy Beast today,
Sleeping peacefully as clear as day,
Its beautiful red coat as bright as the sun,
Although sleeping in the background, a hum
From its monstrous insides, even its tum
Was setting off that terrible hum,
Then expectedly, suddenly,
Its eyes as glittering as diamonds seen,
Started up, not very carefully,
Its monstrous growl and roar and shout
Its shout as loud as a lion's roar,
Its speed as quick as a cheetah galore.
When it was set free its shout as loud as a lion's roar
Got much louder, more, more, more!
Its legs as quick as the speed of light
It gave everybody a fright.
It shot down the road like a thunderstorm
It's luxury out of its form.

James Roy (11)
Henley-In-Arden High School

The Willow Tree

I am the willow tree
My branches, long and thin
My trunk as sturdy as a rock
I drape them down as a dome of leaves.
The light shines through in just small beams
Summer is when I am at my best.
Bright green leaves and all the rest.
I hide the children as they play.
I am so strong they swing on rope-like branches
Until snap!
One has come off, oh, just the kids.
But then another and then another.
It is pruning time.
Games are over.
They build something, it is a fire of my branches.
Out the stack my summer goes.
Up in smoke for now it is winter.

And that is the end of my day.

David Follows (11)
Henley-In-Arden High School

THE GAME

This is the day.
I've been waiting for a week!
Come on boys.
Let's get dressed, kick some butt!
I put on my shorts
Then my top.
I struggle with my shin pads,
I struggle with my socks,
But my football boots slip right on.
I get mud and grass all over myself
My players don't pass much,
But I sure get a kick.
By the time we have finished the pitch looks like me.

Michael Collins (12)
Henley-In-Arden High School

THAT'S THE WAY I AM

I'm walking down the road one day
Feeling sad and blue.
Thinking of myself of course,
But that's the thing I do

Never to think of my friends or family
Thinking of myself again,
But that's the thing I do

I'm walking to my house
Feeling sad and blue
Wondering what to say to my mum
For being late from school

I wonder if she will tell me off,
But that's not my fault
All I am doing is learning my spellings
And thinking of myself

I have just opened the door
Feeling sad and blue
Thinking about myself again
And to remember to think of you.

Meg Caple (12)
Henley-In-Arden High School

My Day

When I get up
I eat my breakfast
Then brush my teeth.
I wash my face
And brush my hair
I put my clothes on
Then walk to the bus stop
Have a long journey
And then get off
Walk into school
Go to form
Then go to lesson
First is PE
Doing some rugby
Running in and out
Have a break
Play football with my friends
Then have some lunch
And back to lessons
Get back on the bus
Until I get home!

Alex Unitt (11)
Henley-In-Arden High School

RABBITS

My rabbit is really fun,
it hops around in its run.

Some rabbits are very big,
my rabbit loves to dig.

Some rabbits are white,
mine sleeps in its cage at night.

Its tail looks like a ball,
and also is very small.

I brought my rabbit from a farm,
I carry it round in my arms.

My rabbit has a big tummy,
and is always very funny.

Gillian Grandfield (11)
Henley-In-Arden High School

MY RAIN POEM

That rain, that rain, has come again,
Drip, drop, down the drain it goes again,
Faster and faster it goes,
I hate the rain!
Down it goes from the sky,
I'm watching from the windowpane,
The drips are having a race down the windowpane,
I hate the rain!
Things outside getting wet,
Mum's left the roof off the car,
I hate the rain!
I can hear it on the old roof top,
I want to go outside,
And splish, splash in those big puddles,
I hate the rain, the rain, the rain!

Harry Skelton (12)
Henley-In-Arden High School

A Poem About Me!

About me,
I like to start the day with toast and tea,
Most mornings down the road I fly,
To catch my bus for Henley High.

At school I have many friends,
Some I meet at weekends,
I like maths, art and PE,
But not so keen on RE.

My hobbies are skateboarding, F1 and football,
The team I support is Aston Villa,
I go and watch on Saturdays,
Sometimes the match can be a bit of a thriller.

I live with my father and mother,
And little sister and brother,
We have a tank full of fish,
And four little hamsters with a home quite swish.

I play football for Wellsbourne Wanderers,
On Sundays we travel near and far,
For teams we try to beat,
Which is no mean feat.

So this is a poem about me,
This is all for now as Mum's just shouted me for tea.

Ben Shirley-Lobb (11)
Henley-In-Arden High School

FEAR

A scene of death
beneath my chest
Hurtling through my mind
A scent of blood
Then a tremendous thud
On the tiled floor
A figure emerged
With a horrible face
Growling like a wolf
His fangs they bled
For he had fed on poor Uncle Ned.

Ryan Manton (11)
Henley-In-Arden High School

THE SLASH OF A KNIFE

The night was black
and the wind was cold
and a man stood with his knife.
The lightning struck
and the thunder roared
waiting for the man to take his life.

As he waited to fight
he looked around
and something caught his eye.
He charged straight up
to see what it was
then he slashed it with his knife.

Then he ran to hide
and watch his prey,
but then it got up and said
'I can't be killed
you stupid fool'
As he watched his deadly dead.

Emma Johnson (11)
Henley-In-Arden High School

SPOOKY POEM

The night was black
And there was a moon
That shone on a tomb
Human or beast, the secret lay in a sack.

It lay in the darkness for many years
At last it is revealed,
But here comes someone brave
And they stand next to the grave.

Ben Jennings (11)
Henley-In-Arden High School

SPOOKY POEM

The night was black
The hair stood up on my back
The floorboards creaked
As I sneaked
A spooky sound came from the ground
And a smell that came from Hell
Bang, bang, bang!
Clang, clang, clang!
It became cold
And I was shaky
A ghost appeared
With a dirty, grey beard
Boooo!
And it went into my body
And I was no more!

David Dellenty (11)
Henley-In-Arden High School

A Ghost With A Grudge

A ghoulish house,
A midnight fear,
The squeak of a mouse,
Down trickles a tear.

Heavy lies the mist,
A ghost in armour,
A moral with a twist,
This ghost needs to be calmer.

His victim is dead,
This ghost is mad,
A bullet through the head,
Alas, the tale is sad.

So pale he lays,
Now where's his wife?
Gone are his days,
Been slit with a knife.

Away the ghost flew,
Without a care in the world
Galloping through the rustling trees.

Now everyone knows
So keep well clear,
Be on your toes,
Oh dear, oh dear, oh dear!

Felicity Wright (11)
Henley-In-Arden High School

11TH SEPTEMBER

It happened on a Tuesday, the day that shook the world,
People watched in total disbelief as tragedies unfurled.
The day began like any other, no one knew what was to come,
People went about their business; inside school, office or home.

The World Trade Center's twin towers, stretched skyward,
proud and tall,
A striking feature of the skyline, recognised by one and all.
A symbol of the free world, America's financial core,
A target for extremists plotting murderous acts of war.

A plane packed full of passengers, but with terrorists in control
Flew straight into one tower and left a gaping hole,
The fuel exploded, hundreds died, horrific scenes of devastation.
What victims suffered is beyond belief and contemplation.

Minutes later, frightened eyes watched as a second hijacked plane
Collided with the second tower, causing suffering and pain.
The world could not believe what it was witnessing first hand -
How could this all be happening in this powerful free land?

But more was still to come and right before our very eyes,
The towers collapsed and death came falling from the darkened skies.
In the aftermath that followed people ran and people screamed,
This sickening, living nightmare worse than anyone had dreamed.

Blood and bodies, dust and debris, shock and panic everywhere,
Federal agents, police and firemen, heroic acts from those who care.
The President has pledged that those responsible will pay,
The FBI will find them, they can't hide or run away.

But for now we must remember those whose lives have been cut short,
And pray for their friends and families, while justice is swiftly sought.
And hope that from the rubble and the ashes that remain
Will come for all a symbol of peace and freedom once again.

Hannah Alexander (13)
Henley-In-Arden High School

DOOMSDAY

It feels like World War III began today,
distress, devastation, fear, misery.
The plane approached the tower,
like a thundering rhino charging at its foe.
Flames roared bright orange and yellow,
like the burning breath of a dragon.
The building was crumbling away piece by piece.
Two blocks stood tall and strong but now lay in ashes.
The usual busy hub of New York City has turned
into a stunned silence.
A shadow of dust fills the 'Big Apple' like icing
on a cake.
Thousands of innocent lives taken, meaningless
murderers on a suicide mission,
21st Century was supposed to have been a new beginning,
not the end.
A frantic search for survivors,
Three hundred firemen, eighty policemen,
mothers, fathers, friends and loved ones.
So many people have died. How should
someone respond to something so gruesome?
Revenge must be taken!

Emily Styles (13)
Henley-In-Arden High School

SO MUCH FOR A NORMAL DAY

Wake up, everything is fine,
New York's Twin Towers stand proud across the skyline.
People yawn, begin to wake up and say,
Guess it's another start to a normal day.
Everyone carries on unaware,
No one knows what will happen next up there.
Crash! Bang! A hole appears,
Nobody dares to go near.
An accident, yes, that's what they decide,
But another plane goes through the other tower's side.
Surely there can be another way?
No, so much for a normal day.
The Pentagon, the Americans' army base,
Is half destroyed as if it were paste.
The White House is evacuated straightaway,
So much for a normal day.
The last of four hijacked planes
Crashes in Pennsylvania in smoke and flames.
It's a terrorist's game of cat and mouse,
But in this game some people can't go hide in their house.
So much for a normal day.

Hannah Emm (13)
Henley-In-Arden High School

THE NEW EVIL IN OUR WORLD!

Clouds of smoke, erupting fireballs
Cause shattered lives and devastation
It isn't fair, it isn't right.
Is it war? Will we fight?

Rubble and debris pour as rain
Huge explosions from within
Like a horror movie, it can't be real
Who would want this pain and fear?

Alive is the evil in our world
Can we kill it? Will it die?
Dead are the victims, lost forever
Gone is the landscape blown from the sky.

What can we do? How can we help?
Is there hope, can He hear our prayers?
Can it worsen? Surely not
We must do something, let us try

America wants some justice
Or is it just revenge?
We all need some answers
Who? How and why?

Sam Williams (13)
Henley-In-Arden High School

BALLAD POEM
*(Based on Hannah and Joe Brown from
Laurie Lee's 'Cider with Rosie')*

Hannah and Joe lived deep in Slad.
They loved the life they had.
Their sons and daughters moved away.
They never bothered anyway.

Hannah, she would wash and cook.
Joe chopped wood with a billhook.
They ate fruit so they wouldn't get ill,
But they did it with skill.

Feebleness knocked them on the floor.
They couldn't live anymore.
Neighbours got worried and called round.
Saw them on the ground.

The authorities were told
By someone cold.
The spinster said they would be moved
Somewhere to get food.

The workhouse is where they would be sent
Later that day they went.
A grey shadow closed on their life
Joe would lose his wife.

They were told they would see each other twice a week,
But Joe wouldn't keep.
The workhouse was their worst fear
After fifty years.

They wouldn't see each other again
They separated wondering when
A week later they began to weep.
They died in their sleep.

All that remained of their life before.
Was rubble on the floor.

Christopher Harrold (13)
Henley-In-Arden High School

ONE ANSWER

They crashed down,
helpless, falling,
unknowingly shattering bones,
shattering lives.

Helicopters, circling, helpless,
watching people jump to their deaths,
trying to save themselves,
to warn us.

The Pentagon also suffered great fate,
just after the towers,
maiming people with its
scorching flames of Hell.

Relatives cried and screamed,
one plane, an accident,
two? Three?
What could it mean?

The Apocalypse? No.
A war? Who knows?
Maybe there is only one answer -
Revenge?

Nicola Guest (14)
Henley-In-Arden High School

AN ABNORMAL DAY IN THE PERFECT WORLD?

People unaware of real destruction,
Trading in the tremendous Twin Towers
People boarding their own country's jets
Surely no hijacking in the US?
Planes in a kamikaze flight round the Earth
Destruction. Destruction that's on the cards.

Diving furiously, turning wildly
Crash went one,
Bang went the other
Flames ran from floor to floor
Killing everyone from large to small.

The Pentagon in pride of place
Wasn't it the Ministry of Defence?
Five-sided now, down to three
Total destruction in Washington DC.

Twin Towers stand so proud
Taller than skyscrapers, wider than seas
Flat as a pancake in just thirteen minutes
Destroying people's dreams, crushing their families
Who deserves this tragic fate?
New York skyline never to be right.
Terrorists make the world take fright!

James Follows (13)
Henley-In-Arden High School

Guilt

Why did you have to do it?
To take them all yourself?
Fathers, grandparents, cousins, mothers.
You killed them all yourself.

Why did you have to make it?
To make the rage complete?
You sucked it up and then crushed them
                          beneath your feet.
All of them.

I suppose you had to do it
To make yourself heard.
But other people's ideas
Didn't get to your ears.

Ideas, wants, needs . . .
Personalities.
Are your path.
To what you want.

You are the one who makes the choice.
The one who had a voice.
The one who gave all he had.
To start us going mad!

All the buildings but none.
Many feelings gone.
Many emotions heard.
Death was your mask.

So if I could meet you now.
Look at you face to face.
You stand upon your rebel base.
I ask you . . . .why?

Who are you?

Philip Inman (13)
Henley-In-Arden High School

Two Tallest Buildings

A few days ago where busy bods meet,
Stood two tallest buildings on a Manhattan street.
A low flying plane catches corners of eyes
The sound of the explosion, muffled by cries.
What a horrible, terrible, horrific mistake.
Then comes the next shock, bringing more heartache.
Second plane glides towards the neighbouring tower.
Hitting the side with almighty power.
People screaming everywhere.
No one to help! Everyone to care!
South Tower crumbles down and down.
In the rubble is where people drown.
People look on in desperate fright.
Will it be over by the end of the night?
Then goes the North Tower as fast as the first.
Terrorists are the people the world will curse.
Mourning families and crying friends.
Journalists and photographers see through the lens.
Rising dust hanging over New York.
Two tallest building now turned to chalk.
What was achieved by this psychotic act?
Apart from the lives that thousands now lack!

Laura Robertson (13)
Henley-In-Arden High School

OUR ENGLISH TEACHER

Our English teacher, Mr Paine
He loves World Cup '94
He also loves Star Trek
'Cause he's got posters on the door.

His favourite team is Coventry
He wears fantastic ties
And when he says Star Trek is good
It's all a pack of lies.

He wears bright-coloured shirts
Orange, yellow and pink
And when he's teaching us a lesson
It's very hard to think.

Chris Smith (13)
Light Hall School

FRIENDS

I'd like to introduce you,
To some very good friends of mine,
If you've got the place,
Then I've got the time,

To tell you about Joey,
He's dim yet cute,
As thick as a door post,
But good looks to boot,

Followed by Phoebe,
A good-hearted airhead,
She's the resident flake,
With a mother who's dead,

Then there's Ross,
He's been married thrice,
And all his wives,
Are extremely nice,

There's also Rachel,
She worked at Central Perk,
But now she's into fashion,
And always late for work,

Could he be more adorable?
Next is Chandler,
He's a Baywatch scholar,
The wisecracking computer programmer,

Last is Monica,
She's neurotic and quirky,
A compulsive chef,
Famous for her turkey.

Charlotte Wakelyn (13)
Light Hall School

DREAMS

Dreams are lovely places
A wonderful fantasy in your head
They fill your brain with pretty pictures
Whilst you are in bed.

You dream whilst you are asleep
Sometimes you toss and turn
Some people dribble
And some people snore.

But not all dreams are good
Some of them can scare you
Try not to think about bad things before
you go to sleep at night
Think good things and you will be all right.

Rebecca Partridge (13)
Light Hall School

THE DEVIL, GOD AND YOU

The Devil and God, do they exist?
Fathers and priests do persist
To make us believe that they do
'No matter what, they're watching you.'
They say be good, go to Heaven,
Past Cloud 9 and up through 11.
They say be bad go to Hell
The fiery place where no one does well.
So do they exist? You decide,
And prepare yourself now for the
                              Afterlife ride!

Harry Minton (13)
Light Hall School

The Villa Poem

At the beginning of the season,
We looked for
A decent run in Europe,
Or perhaps the FA Cup!

Merson is usually designing,
Moustapha Hadji is our best signing,
We make teams look very boring
While Juan Pablo is up front scoring

In the stands we have our fans,
Eating pies and drinking from cans,
When we score Gregory goes on a run,
But he doesn't give the players much fun!

David Alford (13)
Light Hall School

YOUR MAGICAL LIFE

Little child, make a wish,
Believe in yourself and the magic you give,
Don't grow too fast,
Make all the fun last,
And enjoy the life that you live.

If things ever go bad,
Don't be too sad,
There's a way to make it better,
If you try to make it better,
And the pain will fade away.

Hold your head up high,
Don't let life go by,
Always stay strong,
Life can never be too long,
Lock all your happiness inside your head.

Lorna Rosie (13)
Light Hall School

AMERICA

It was an ordinary day
Until the towers came crashing down
Smoke was everywhere
People were running through the town

It was terrible
When the plane hit the tower
It was then I realised
The terrorists had the power

I watched as the shock
Spread throughout the world
And as the Twin Towers just
Hurtled and hurtled

Down they came
Crashing and booming
Everyone just kept
Assuming . . .

The best of things,
But that'll never come
Of this terrible tragedy
What's done is done!

Amy Gardiner (14)
Light Hall School

A Poem For America!

The whole world's been affected
In many different ways;
Loss of friends and family
All in just one day.

Pictures of the tragic events
Keep running through my mind;
The hurt, the pain, the terror
How could anyone be so unkind?

Leaving New York in clouds of smoke
And the world in devastation;
News on the dreadful attack
Has spread throughout the nation.

So please Lord hear my prayer
I promise I won't lose faith;
But please grant me this favour
And keep the whole world safe . . .

From war, from pain, from anger,
From rage, regret and hate;
I wish the world could get along
Wouldn't it just be great?

Donna Organ (13)
Light Hall School

LIVING ON THE STREETS

What is it like, to live on the street?
No clothes to wear, or shoes on your feet
Nobody looks, not even a glare
Sometimes it's like, you're not even there
You are moved on from every place
By any person, of any race
You carry a bag, it's your abode
Take it with you as you wander the roads
What is it like, to live on the street?
No clothes to wear, or shoes on your feet.

Stefan Nowakowski (13)
Light Hall School

Did You Know That...

A is for Anthea who turns out the lights,
B is for Barry who fights and bites,
C is for Claire who has blonde hair,
D is for Dave who is unfair,
E is for Esther who has a big nose,
F is for Frank who likes to pose,
G is for Gladys who has lots of money,
H is for Harry who eats lots of honey,
I is for Irene who owns a big house,
J is for Joe who has a pet mouse,
K is for Kate who eats lots of cake,
L is for Liam who jumped in the lake,
M is for Michelle who grows big flowers,
N is for Norris who has super powers,
O is for Olivia who collects different bugs,
P is for Peter who has dirty 'lugs',
Q is for Queenie who tells lots of lies,
R is for Robert who ate all the pies,
S is for Sophie who has lots of keys,
T is for Tom who is allergic to cheese,
U is for Ursula who has an empty purse,
V is for Victor who drives a hearse,
W is for Wendy who draws on walls,
X is for Xander who runs in the halls,
Y is for Yasmine who can't stand the boys,
And Z is for Zack who plays with his toys.

Sophie Priestley (13)
Light Hall School

HAVE YOU EVER BEEN TO THE ZOO BEFORE?

'Have you ever been to the zoo before?'
'No, not really, I've heard it's all a bore.'
'There's lions, giraffes and plenty to do.'
'I don't think I've heard of it, is it new?'
'The monkeys swing from tree to tree,
While the elephants are hoping to be set free.
The tigers are prowling around the cage,
And the lions start to roar with rage.
At twelve o'clock, it's time to be fed . . .
Then before they know it, it's time for bed.
Have you ever been to the zoo before?'

Claire Blake (13)
Light Hall School

Aberfan - A Day Of Terror

One winter's night in Aberfan 1966,
the children played happily together.
No one knew about the tragedy,
that would ruin their lives forever!

As they talked between themselves,
in registration that day.
They heard the rumbling get closer,
as the hill slid away!

But by then it was far too late,
as the damage had already been done.
The school was completely covered,
the battle had already been won!

They were all buried alive,
in such a horrible way.
One hundred and sixteen pupils,
did not return that day!

The community and services,
rushed to the scene.
They could not take in the sight,
where the school had been!

One can't imagine what they must have felt,
no one deserves to die that way.
Their loved ones had gone forever,
it was Aberfan's blackest day!

They helped for the sake of the children,
whose lives now sadly perished.
Just because they themselves have gone,
the memories will always be cherished!

Aberfan - will always be known as a day of terror!

Sarah Morgan (13)
Light Hall School

WINTER

Summer's gone and winter's coming.
Autumn's nearly over,
The leaves are falling red and brown,
Mornings getting colder.

The evenings slowly drawing in,
Mornings just like twilight,
The moon's still out at 8am,
When I wake, it's still not daylight.

Rain will come, together with thunder,
Snow will fall without a sound,
The birds will fly south for sun and heat,
And ice will freeze the ground.

Springtime will come, but go again,
And summer and autumn too,
Then winter will arrive for another time,
And raindrops will fall on you.

Harrie Gibson (13)
Light Hall School

THE NEW YORK TRAGEDY!

It was just another day in the big city
Looked over by the Statue of Liberty
It only took a single sin
To let an awful tragedy begin.

Citizens could only stare
As the plane descended from the air
And as it crashed from the sky
Many people were about to die.

The results of attacks proved a cost
Many people's lives were lost
And all the English and American men
Will make sure this will never happen again.

Tom Fleming (13)
Light Hall School

SCHOOL

School is a place to learn and to play,
Different subjects every day.
Six hours from nine till three,
Some are expensive others are free.

Science can be good when experiments are done,
Technology is OK, when you don't hit your thumb.
Maths is boring, no fun to be had,
English means writing which isn't too bad.

Languages are excellent and not too hard,
Art is making things, sometimes out of card.
In geography you usually study maps,
In drama you pretend to turn on taps.

In music you can play on the keyboard,
RE is mainly studying our Lord.
History's all about things in the past,
Games are races and not coming last.

As you can see school isn't too bad,
Except for when the teachers get mad.
The years you're at school are supposed to be the best,
So make the most of it and pass the test.

Charlotte Holywell (13)
Light Hall School

I'M JUST MAGGIE

My name, it doesn't matter to them,
Our ages, they couldn't care less,
My religion and where I live does,
Now our town and street is a mess.

By the way it's Maggie, aged four, Catholic,
My house is at the top of the Ardoyne Road,
My school, is at the bottom; I hate walking there,
I sometimes pray the Lord will lighten this load.

It starts at night; I hate the noise,
The screaming, shouting, bombing and smashing,
I put my fingers in my ears and hum a tune,
I sometimes cry with fear, it's terrifying.

The following morning the road is deserted,
Glass, brick and burning cars fill the street,
I get dressed, brush my hair, and clean my teeth,
As I stand on my drive my heart skips a beat.

There's a group of us moms, dads and children,
We congregate every morning ready to leave,
The Protestants stand, stare, scream and shout,
One throws a stone; I run, cry, can barely breathe.

They are the Protestants doing this,
Protesting they're hurting with the will the fight,
I try to understand their pain,
I try to see wrong and right.

But after all I'm just Maggie, age four, Catholic,
That doesn't matter; they couldn't care less,
I don't know what I have done wrong,
I'm just a girl in a red and white school dress.

Rebecca Palmer (14)
Light Hall School

THE DOLPHIN

Through harsh waters it slips and slides,
The soft sea spray against its sides,
Its shiny skin of silver grey,
It hunts down its vulnerable prey.
Past cliffs of terracotta clay,
Past jagged rocks before a bay,
It weaves between the water weeds,
And coral reefs to where it feeds.
It dances in the fiery skies,
At sunset and at sunrise.
And day and night its subtle cries,
Echo as the great tide dies.
It spins above the giant waves,
It swims past secret submerged caves,
It sings its song as it is free,
It hides its peace within the sea.

Charlotte Timmons (13)
Light Hall School

MY LITTLE SISTER

I have a little sister,
Who thinks she's Britney Spears,
But no one likes to tell her,
That she really hurts our ears.

I have a little sister,
Who likes to sing and dance,
Her favourite move is the spin,
Which puts me in a trance.

I have a little sister,
Who really likes to shout,
She does it no matter where she is,
Until she gets a clout.

I have a little sister,
Who can be really cute,
But I really hate it when
She decides to play her flute.

I have a little sister,
Who always steals my stuff,
And when I ask her for it back,
She starts to act all tough.

I have a little sister,
Who really likes fancy dress,
She parades the house in Mom's high heels,
Until everyone said
'Look ahhh bless.'

Emma Gunning (13)
Light Hall School

THE LAST MOMENT

I know this is;

My last time to watch
the ripples of the lake,
My last moment to hear what
the tearful birds sing,
My last opportunity to smell
the green wilderness forest,
My last chance to touch
the coarse pine woodland bench,

I count down;

My last day to live my life as it is,
My last hour to consider, the chances,
My last minute to realise
What will happen,
My last second to stand
Up and grip the ground,

And I ask myself,
What have I done with my life?

Rachael A Chadwick (13)
Light Hall School

Love In My Eyes Only

I saw a boy
he made me smile
he gave me happiness all the while.

As I looked into his big blue eyes
I knew I loved him I thought I would die
heart racing
knees shaking
I turned away.

I've never felt like this before
I was new to it all
as time passed I phoned him up
confessed then hung up.

Tomorrow brought another day
I said 'Hi' and he walked away
tears dripped from my eyes
I turned away and said goodbye.

Weeks were spent to make him talk,
but all I got was 'Hi' and 'Bye'
my heart sank and so did I
three words had ruined it all.

Now I know life's unfair
and dreams cannot always be there.

Christine Mackie (13)
Light Hall School

WINTER

Everyone dreams of a snow white ground
In winter
Leaves have gone from all around
In winter

The nights are long, the weather is dull
When winter's here
And soon the shops will be full,
Because Christmas is getting near

The snow can fall, the rain can flood
In winter
Kids play in the soggy mud
In winter

Night-times are cosy and snug
In winter
The dog sits in front of the fire upon the rug
In winter.

Lucy Goldingay (13)
Light Hall School

911

In New York City the sky was blue
The day two planes into the towers flew.
Screams could be heard for miles around,
As the towers crumbled to the ground.
Who caused all this terrorist trouble?
People buried alive under the rubble.
Witnesses and rescuers began to cry
As the smoke and fumes filled the sky.
George Bush is mad and declares a war,
The problem is too great for him to ignore.
So many innocent lives have been lost,
But for the killers it's a small cost.

Gemma Beck (13)
Light Hall School

MY CAT

Big green eyes, trusting you,
Fluffy tail, greeting you,
Four quiet feet, creeping up on you,
Small pink ears, listening for you,

Black, white, brown and ginger,
Black stripes, white tummy, brown tail and ginger spot,
Furry and fluffy, soft and silky,
Furry and fluffy tummy, soft and silky body.

Chewing my bag and attacking the carpet,
Chasing sunbeams and chasing string,
Looking out the window and curling up to sleep,
Eating all the food and sitting on me.

Laura Macdonald (14)
Light Hall School

NO ONE EXPECTED IT TO HAPPEN

No one expected it to happen,
It was just an ordinary day,
People woke up in the morning,
Got dressed and got on their way.

No one expected it to happen,
It was just an ordinary day,
People went to work,
Working to get their pay.

No one expected it to happen,
It was just an ordinary day,
When terror struck America,
In such an awful way.

No one expected it to happen,
It was just an ordinary day,
People are lost forever, (maybe),
It's been such an awful day.

No one expected it to happen,
It was just an ordinary day,
No one should've died,
What did they do, or say?

No one expected it to happen,
It was just an ordinary day,
When terror struck America,
In such an awful way.

No one expected it to happen,
It was just an ordinary day.

Sumitra Oliver (13)
Light Hall School

THE DAY THAT CHANGED THE WORLD

T he day that changed the world,
H ow could we not remember?
E very person who got caught in the flames,

D ied on the 11th September;
A ll the nations were shocked,
Y et they never gave up hope,

T hat is why we will defeat the evil, that
H as caused us all to mope;
A plane from the sky,
T riggered people to run,

C hasing the deadly smoke away,
H aving no sense of what else was to come;
A nd the three other planes descended,
N ot once has the world given up faith,
G od will protect us don't worry,
E very person will be safe;
D isaster was caused by sinister people,

T hat killed themselves so they could break millions of hearts,
H ave also committed mass murder and
E ven broken very important building into millions of parts;

W ill you please bow your heads,
O r just say a sweet loving prayer,
R emembering the innocent people,
L ost in the smoke, because of people who didn't care,
D estroying the lives of many; right out of thin air.

Rebecca Foster (13)
Light Hall School

A LITTLE STING!

As I was walking home from school one day
I found a little thing.
I picked it up and suddenly it gave me a little sting.

My finger started to swell and burn
Oh what had I done now?
I tried to catch this thing, but it just ran off
And gave me a scowl.

I raced home to my mom and bashed down the door.
'Oh Mom, oh Mom my finger's really sore.'

I ran my finger under the tap, but it was still sore,
And then out the corner of my eye I saw two
Of these things climbing up the door!

'Those are the rascals, go on get 'em.'
They flew around in the sky
Oh no they're aiming for Mom's eye!

I pushed my mom out the way
I'd saved her what could I say!

Finally we'd killed them all,
And most of them up the wall.

I feel quite guilty now I've slaughtered them all,
But then 'ping' . . . oh no not more!

Sophie Chalmers (11)
Light Hall School

NIGHT

Night,
Is a kind loving person,
With no face.
He will sing me to sleep,
Like my mum.

Night,
Is like a bird flying across the sky,
Covering the Earth with his dark black cape.

Night,
Makes me feel safe,
And I know that I've got nothing to be
scared about.

Night,
Lives up in the sky,
He will turn around and make the dark sky sparkle.

Night,
Will send shooting stars across the sky
when he is happy,
But when he is sad he will just stay dull
and black.

Night,
Will send you to sleep,
Then he will wake you up before morning comes.

Jennifer Cross (11)
Light Hall School

WHY DID MY MASTER MAKE ME?

Lonely,
On my own,
No one to turn to in a crisis,
Why did my master make me?

Humiliation,
I know why,
I'm totally different to the rest,
Why did my master make me?

Life,
Creation,
Going somewhere where no other human has been before,
That's why my master made me!

Chloe Dale (11)
Light Hall School

MY IMAGINARY FRIEND

I've an imaginary friend his name is *Fred!*
Black hair, size; small, with an enormous *head!*
One day, went out, a game of *basketball!*
Our team lost because Fred is so *small!*
Following that, we had swimming *after!*
Fred got stuck in the shallow end, causing lots if *laughter!*
Fred started talking, the chat came to an *end!*
I got really upset when I found . . . I'm the imaginary *friend!*

Jonathan Dattani (12)
Light Hall School

I Have A Mate Called Ozzy!

I have a mate called Ozzy
He has spiked up hair,
We don't have much in common,
But I like him all the same.

Ozzy is a friendly boy
He'll chat to almost anyone,
Although at times he can be shy,
He's usually the loudest in the group.

Ozzy is a picky eater,
He pecks at all his food,
But then again I suppose he would
After all he's only a cockatiel!

Gregory Day (12)
Light Hall School

SKIING

Skiing can be really fun
Going down a mountain
Until you land on your bum
Then bruises will be sprouting.

Scott Murray (11)
Light Hall School

FOOTBALL

Shooting, passing, goals!
Football is the greatest game
It is fantastic.

Philip Partridge (11)
Light Hall School

THE SPIDER

I am a spider
I live on the ground

On eight legs I scutter
Around and around

In dustbins and drainpipes
I shelter from rain

My family live
In a city in Spain

I travel around
All places I find

Looking for people
I wish they were kind

They try to squash me
I run, try to hide

My best friend money spider
That is how he died

My favourite places
Are in people's baths

When people see me
They scream not laugh

I am a spider
I live on the ground

On eight legs I scutter
Around and around.

Charlotte Wright (11)
Light Hall School

I AM A BT PAYPHONE!

I am a BT payphone,
I hear all your calls.
Love, screams, shouts and pranks,
I hate it when you haul!

I am a nosy payphone,
I eat up all your money!
Some calls make me laugh,
Because you are so funny!

One day a boy came up,
And thought I was a toy!
He pressed my buttons and tickled my tummy,
He also named me Roy!

Another day a man came up,
And asked for his friend Mike.
He was on the phone for quite a while,
Talking about his bike!

I am a BT payphone,
I like to hear you calling.
But only if you're nice and calm,
Not if you're boring!

My final word is just to say
I do quite like my day.
It's fun to be just like me,
Very, very nosy!

Cally Weeks (11)
Light Hall School

Journey To Space

The astronauts get kitted up
They walk into the shuttle
The door behind is then shut
The shuttle starts to rattle

The astronauts must be scared
They slowly lift-off the floor
They soon pick up a lot of speed
They enter space and soar

The giant rocket breaks away
The shuttle aims at the moon
The astronauts see a great array
Of stars they will pass soon

They've taken lots of pictures
And samples of the moon,
But they have to think about
Coming back home soon

They have done their mission
And want to come back home
They get through the atmosphere
And see the Millennium Dome

They get nearer the ground
And see the landing site
Once they have landed
The crowd cheer with delight.

David Yeomans (11)
Light Hall School

CHRISTMAS PRESENTS

It's time for snow!
You ask for a pony for Christmas,
But your parents say *'No!'*
Talk about unfair.

The snow's too low,
You ask for a computer for Christmas,
But your parents say *'No!'*
Talk about unfair.

Your body is freezing, especially your toes,
You ask for a bike for Christmas,
But your parents say *'No!'*
Talk about unfair.

You make a cake with dough,
You ask for a cake baker for Christmas,
But your parents say *'No!'*
Talk about unfair.

Christmas morning is dawning,
What will you get?
A TV, a radio,
Or a cutlery set?

You get up, your room is a mess!
You get a lump of coal,
You ask if it is a joke,
And your parents say *'Yes!'*

You get a bike, you get a bird,
You even get lemon curd,
You thank your mom, you thank your dad,
This is the best Christmas you've ever had!

Charlotte Sewell (11)
Light Hall School

A Wolf In Winter

Sad winter and darkening nights,
snuggle up out go the lights,
Rest your head and close your eyes,
put all your thoughts and troubles aside.

Yet no one knows what waits in the dark,
beyond the woods in the endless dark
and no one knows what waits in the trees,
waiting, just waiting in the silent breeze.

All is quiet nothing stirs,
nothing sounds and I hear no birds,
yet somewhere out there in the woods,
I saw a creature, there it stood.

He started creeping and crawling along,
with his legs so sturdy and so strong,
he looks around as he hunts,
searching for hours for his lunch.

As he stares up at the late full moon,
he knows the neighbourhood will be awakening soon,
the cover of darkness will soon cease
he prays all mankind will leave him in peace.

Megan Timmons (11)
Light Hall School

IN THE DARK OF THE NIGHT

In the dark of the night,
Where nothing could be seen,
From over the hills, a clipity clop,
A lonesome shadow once had been.

Some knight in armour appeared on a horse,
I saw him then blinked,
But then he was gone,
All that was heard in the dark of the night,
Was a distant sound, a view of none.

Again the next night,
I returned to the scene,
When the mist came down, I waited alone,
Where the knight and his horse had once been.

My luck had run out,
I waited all night for the shadow to appear,
No sounds could be heard,
By now I was cold and even shed a tear.

I made my way home,
Sad and upset,
But at least I had a memory of the shadow that night,
The knight and his horse, that once I had met.

Stephanie Perrin (11)
Light Hall School

DOES SANTA .. ?

Does Santa Claus have a beard,
As white as the fluffy snow?
Jack Frost is always feared,
In case he keeps Santa away.

Does Santa have a herd of deer,
As soft as my teddy bear?
Their eyes are ever so clear,
What a lovely heard of deer.

Does Rudolph have a red nose,
So bright it can guide you along?
He stands and does a pose,
With is bright red, glowing nose.

Does Father Christmas have a wife?
Is she nice and warm and cuddly?
Does she cut food with a knife,
Or does she make wonderful cookies?

Does Santa have a lovely red hat
All fluffy and floppy?
Is he very chubby and fat?
Does he wear a red hat?

But the main thing lots of people want to know
Is quite a big question,
It's not to learn how to sew
But is Father Christmas real?

Samantha-Ann Medlicott (11)
Light Hall School

IMAGINARY WORLD

To my darling diary Di,

Last night I crept into Anne's dream
It was about this boy,
'That secret's safe with me,' I said,
'You'd like him too!' she cried.

Today I went to school with Anne
I helped her with her sums
I saw a boy who's really cool,
But he cannot see me.

Anne wanted to go to space today,
So we grabbed a cardboard box.
I waved my wand and winked my eye
The box is now a spaceship!

Today I rate nine out of ten
So goodbye darling Di.
I'll write in you tomorrow of course
Love dearly from
Imogen Friend
xxx

PS: I wonder what rating
I would receive
For being Anne's imaginary friend.

Judith Dray (11)
Light Hall School

FEATHER OF DEATH

'A big brave Barbarian'
Said all the village
He's off to kill the Dragon Lord
In the dark cave

As he arrived flames came out
Of the big, dark cave,
But then he heard a big *'Aaaachhoo'*
And out came another blast

So he entered big and brave
He drew his sword in his trembling hands,
But he kept moving
As he entered the main hall
He saw a dragon big and tall,

But then he was blown away
By a big *Aaacchhhooo!*

But he came back struggling and asked the dragon
'What is wrong Dragon Lord?' he asked
'I've got the sneezes' the dragon replied

'I know!' said the Barbarian, 'I'll stick my sword up your nose and have a look.'
So he did and out popped a littler feather
Then the dragon ate the Barbarian

So the villagers said 'Poor dead, dead, dead Barbarian.'

Samuel Drage (11)
Light Hall School

CATS

Cats are hungry
Eating all day
Then they sleep
Within the hay

Farm cats chase mice
Always on the prowl
Teatime is coming
With the hoot of the owl

Persian cats are matted
Give them lots of fuss
What shall we call him?
How about Tubby puss!

Manx cats are cheeky
They have no tails
They love lots of games
Like chasing the mail!

Siamese are show-offs
The best of the lot
Do you think they're normal?
They're certainly not

Now you see
Cats are the best pets
They'll love you forever
Do you want a bet?

Lynsey Edensor (11)
Light Hall School

MY CHOCOLATE ECLAIR

There was a piece of chocolate,
I stuck it to the floor,
My long lost eclair from the year before.
Next to it I found on the brand new carpet
My ant infested apple core
Pink and green and brown
Ow! The ant just bit me
I cursed it and swore.
Guess what else I found?
The mouse which my cat killed,
Back in nineteen ninety-four.
I found a bit of fishcake,
It had a lot of mould,
Needed a bin to put it in,
But this I could not find.
There was a piece of chocolate
I stuck it to the floor
My mother found me doing it
I shan't do it any more.

Jessica Franklin (12)
Light Hall School

IMAGINING THINGS

Monsters think I'm stupid
Knocking at my door
'Trick or treat?' they say,
But I know they're after more

They killed my mom when I was three
They killed my dad when I was four
Then they tried to kill my cat
And now they're after me

Monsters think I'm stupid
Knocking at my door
'Trick or treat?' they say,
But I know they're after more

They haunt me in my classroom
They haunt me in my bed
They haunt all day long
They're always in my head

Monsters think I'm stupid
Knocking at my door
'Trick or treat?' they say,
But I know they're after more.

Dale Gilbert (11)
Light Hall School

A Terrorist Attack

As the towers fell to the ground
It made a thud and an almighty sound
America stood filled with fear
As they collapsed really near
Every American had a tear in their eye
And the whole world let out a sigh
'Who did this? Where are they?'
'Just you wait till another day!'
Now we're going into war
This will last for ever more!

Daniel Antony Hughes (11)
Light Hall School

A Dull Day

It's dark and windy
The rain is falling
The leaves are scattered about

The trees are bending
The fences are breaking
Watch out we're in for a storm

I'm stuck inside
There's nothing to do
I wish I could go out to play

I miss my friends
From down at the park
This has been a very long day.

Joe Hunt (11)
Light Hall School

THE SURFER

Waiting for a green wave
the surfer waits with caution.
Suddenly the wave approaches
climbing higher and higher.
The surfer paddles and off he goes
riding the wave

The green wave breaking
The surfer skims the azure wave.
Darting in and out trying to find a wave
to do some awesome stunts
Tail whip, DK snap, 360, 180,
and the famous 'air'.

The wave is calming down
He's got no more room for tricks
but he carries on going into the rocks.

Callum Lyall (11)
Light Hall School

A Moonlit Night

The moonlit night that filled the air
And glistens on the trees,
They all droop, short and bare
And rustle with the breeze.

Nothing moves, nothing stirs,
Under that moonlit sky,
But something moves in those icy firs,
Whilst you are passing by.

Questions appear and fill your head,
It's like a story, something you've read,
Someone waiting, waiting for you,
Ready to jump out and scare you . . . *Boo!*

You try to run, try to hide,
Scared through and through,
You stand there think you're safe in this bizarre ride,
But then you see it . . . heading for you!

Alice Hyde (12)
Light Hall School

TESTS

As I sit at my desk,
my hand starts to shake,
out in front of me lies my first test.

My heart starts to race,
as I turn the first page,
my friend seems so cool as I glance at her face.

I look at the question - it's not too bad
I move onto the next,
it's quite easy, I was so glad.

After thirty minutes I've finished it,
I start to stand up,
but my teacher says 'Sit.'

After two weeks had gone,
I got my results,
in the test, I had shone.

Hannah Bluck (11)
Light Hall School

THE FOOTBALL MATCH

Excitement builds
Out come the players
Gleaming new kit
Puddles in goal mouths
Fans waving to the players
Excellent saves
New kit getting extremely muddy
Dirty two-footed challenge
'Penalty!' cries the crowd
'Pheeewp!' goes the ref's whistle
'Goal!' scream the fans
'Pheeewp!' goes the final whistle
1-0 We won!

Chris Carter (11)
Light Hall School

FOOTBALL CRAZY

The start of a fresh new season,
Walking out on the pitch in a gleaming new kit,
The kit soon dirty because of the puddles in goal mouths,
With ball marks on heads, knees and elbows covered in dirt,
While making that reckless tackle in the area, from which they score,
The stinging grass burns from which you made the desperate tackle.

The vibration in your body when you hit the ground with a thud,
And the anger you feel boils up inside you, when the opposition score,
Plus the crunching sliding tackle you made on their left winger,
They score again and you're mad and want revenge,
But then you have hope, but you missed the penalty,
It can't get much worse if the opposition's six foot player
Studs you in your knee.

But the pain, anger and you missing a penalty in the last minute,
Is all worthy at the end of the season, when you win the cup,
And diving head first into the mud,
When you've just scored the winning goal in the final.

Chris Cannon (12)
Light Hall School

LIBERTY'S LOSS

I had seen them coming from miles away,
Like birds descending on their pray.
Soaring through the air at fatal speed,
Before ploughing into the towers like a swimmer into the sea.
Then, with an almighty explosion, the city around me began to panic,
Their screams reverberated through my chambers,
While my heart shuddered as I saw people plunging to their death.
I could not believe my eyes when the towers began to crumble,
I knew that thousands would be dead and buried.
Their families distraught and searching for answers.
I, too, was searching for answers,
However, my question is simple - *why?*
Now there is just a gap where they used to be -
A gap in my life and a gaping wound in my heart.

Caroline Hartley (14)
Saint Martin's School For Girls

CERTAIN DEATH

Given two choices,
Death at both doors.
The rescue a hope,
A dream far away.

The drop deep below me,
Blurring my vision.
The smoke choking my thoughts,
It delays my decision.

My family will wait,
Not knowing my fate.
Living in false hope,
Until my body is found.

Uncertainty remains,
My question begs an answer.
To drop, to die,
To burn alive.

Hannah Tildesley (14)
Saint Martin's School For Girls

HEIGHT OF DESPAIR

Flames of wrath,
Flames of vengeance,
With one terrible act,
Two towers fall,
A symbol of a world divided.
A nation mourns,
A world awaits,
Hoping for a better dawn.
Children cry and families grieve,
Such hatred is hard to conceive.
Many people flee for their lives,
Some confused and others dazed.
Smoke and tears choke the nation,
A skyline changed,
A world in conflict,
The final outcome is yet unknown.
We pray to God for all lives lost,
We pray to God to save our own.

Natalie Carr (14)
Saint Martin's School For Girls

Forever

The carrion of death comes to all,
On the wings of a silver plane it came to pass,
That the twins that dominate the sky should fall.
To the searchers, staring glass-eyed, and scrabbling in the rubble
For the remains of those who are loved but lost
And those who caused their deaths.
Who would have thought such towers could fall?
No one, but those of evil mind whose actions will be
Remembered forever.

Sarah Curtis (14)
Saint Martin's School For Girls

THE FACE OF A MAN

The face of a man with a family and friends,
But he gave it all up for sweet revenge.
The face of a man so fanatical, so obsessed,
That he gave his own life to kill thousands of others.
The face of a man hiding such anger, such hate,
That he truly believed that murder was right.
The face of a man who wanted vengeance so badly,
That he massacred the innocent and devastated the world.
The face of a man who is judged and despised,
But who gave his life for his beliefs and his country.
The face of a man who is cold-hearted and evil
Or the face of a martyr who is courageous and fearless?

Rosie Johnson (14)
Saint Martin's School For Girls

A Journey Through Death

Paralysed, in partial isolation,
Aware of my surroundings,
Using an unknown sense about my person.
Constant flashbacks,
And pictures of my life being played in my head.

Murmurs and comforting words being whispered in my ear,
Unsure of whether I will get the message,
I cry out in silence,
Wanting them to know I love them.
Beep, beep, beep. The end.

Laura Hanlon (14)
Saint Martin's School For Girls

Prima Facie

The scene cries out. They are healing their perpetual scars.
If ignorance is bliss, then does retribution have no meaning?
Guilt overpowers feelings of grief for those of blood family,
and those who were not, but seemed to become it.
Where they stood, a cruel change has taken place,
that we cannot rectify no matter how hard we cry for
their immortality, grieve for their souls or dig until
we ourselves can rest in peace.
Remorse is written on their sorrowful faces,
seen in their movements and shining through their untelling eyes.
Hope is seen as a sponge, now filled with the solidarity
shared by each and every mourner.

The remains sway motionlessly in the chillingly cold wind.
It was to be a beautiful mourning.

Impetuous behaviour is harmful and unwelcome here.
Patience is a virtue in the graveyard of the innocent souls.
They looked on them, expressing words of hope,
praying silently and telling them,
I am coming for you . . .

Knowledge says, there is no doubt it will be a long way
back to the past, but it is on that road that we must
stumble and bear each other to prepare ourselves for
whatever dreams may come.

Mary-Anne McEvilly (14)
Saint Martin's School For Girls

UNDER THE SHADOW OF DEATH

As I flew towards the ground,
Rotating, wheeling round and round,
I thought only of this . . .
All of the things I was going to miss.

I thought of my home, my country,
All the things it had done for me,
Story by story, down I fly,
More terrified people do I pass by.

Distant screams echo through the air,
Any more I cannot bear.
Memories flash through my mind,
The things I love I'll leave behind.

I think of the future - what lies ahead,
Presumably a lot more of this bloodshed.
I only wish I could not have died,
Without saying finally - goodbye.

As the blood rushes to my head,
I think of family and friends instead,
As I see the ground in front of me loom,
It opens up before me - forever my tomb.

Theodora Manassieva (14)
Saint Martin's School For Girls

THE DRAGON OF DEATH

Like a dragon soaring towards its prey it swooped upon me.
Every inch of my being was trying to escape the peril of
its fire-breathing jaws.
But my fate was out of my control,
It had already been determined.

My world was shaken as though a thousand's cannons
Had been blasted through my body.
My senses were drenched with the stench of death,
The blackness of suffering and the raw cold-bloodedness of evil.
A numb disbelief engulfed my mind,
I tried to search for an explanation through the shock,
But drew none.
I felt as if my body had been overtaken by a power
I could not comprehend.

I was falling through space out of control with no sense of being.
It was as if I was being pulled through a black hole.
I no longer had any sense of where I was.
I felt as if my body was gone and only my mangled spirit was left.
As suddenly as a snake striking,
My life was snatched from my grasp
And I fell into the jaws of my dragon.

Claire Hall (14)
Saint Martin's School For Girls

A Glimmer Of Hope

Amidst the atmosphere of death, horror, devastation and grief,
Comes a glimmer of hope,
Like a chink of light through the curtain of darkness.
A time for a moment's celebration.
Searching through the constant reminders of tragedy.
Vainly,
Endlessly,
Hour upon hour,
Day and night,
Searching for someone, somewhere,
Who may have miraculously survived against all odds,
In this almost infinite wreckage,
This total carnage,
This holocaust,
This horror to beat all horrors,
A sign of life,
Five men,
Firefighters,
Frantically uncovered,
Emerged,
Disorientated, but breathing.
A moment's hope to hold on to.

Katherine Morton (14)
Saint Martin's School For Girls

The Beast

Like a fiery ball its head springs up from the ground,
But not making a single sound.
It slowly opens up and opens its head,
Its roots buried deep below buried in their bed.

Its head surrounded by a bright orange mane,
The light reflecting off it from the window pane.
The proud leaves reaching up, stretching,
Bearing their sharp weapons made for scratching.

Basking, stretched in the sun,
Enjoying the warmth, no jobs to be done.
Night falls and it slowly creeps home,
No sound to be heard just the night's gentle moan.

Nicola Porter-Smith (14)
Saint Martin's School For Girls

WHY DID THEY HAVE TO DIE?

A scream, a moan, a whimper, a cry,
The unanswered question - will I live, or will I die?
The images swim madly round his head,
Quivering with confusion, he's filled with fear and dread.

Eyes and lungs filled with thick, grey smoke,
He coughs and splutters - starts to choke.
He has to get out - and it has to be now,
He realises that, but he doesn't know how.

Panic rises, he's shaken to the core,
As he hurriedly searches for the emergency door.
As he exits the building, glad to be alive,
He looks up to see someone balancing - about to dive.

'No!' he screams, his emotions crumbling,
But it's too late, the frightened victim is in the air - tumbling.
He looks round, sees the firemen, his head is spinning,
They're trying to help, but no one is winning.

Memories of the past flash before his eyes,
His wife's sweet smile, his baby's cries.
The happy times they'd shared together,
Would now be lost for ever and ever.

The streets are crowded, full of panic,
Pushing, shoving, all is manic.
He runs for his life, doesn't look back,
Suddenly, the ground beings to shake, and then . . . *black.*

Laura White (14)
Saint Martin's School For Girls

STARS AND STRIPES

Amidst the pain and betrayal,
Rises a phoenix from the flames.
Shooting stars ascend towards the sky,
The American flag is raised.

It flutters like a sail on a ship,
Leading to new horizons.
However, the sail will only function
If wind, behind it, whirls.

Up and up it climbs,
As all fell down before.
All the structural damage,
is comparatively easy to restore.

As we look back with horror and anguish,
We have to establish why,
Confront the problem face on -
But never be ashamed to cry.

Hannah Mansfield (14)
Saint Martin's School For Girls

UNDER SHADOWS OF DARKNESS

A cloud of thick smoke,
This isn't a joke,
As the tower comes down,
It causes a frown,
Collapses around them
And tries to drown them.

Emergency services are here,
Firemen with little fear,
A sight of destruction,
The chief gives instruction,
The men move in,
Work will begin.

As the weather gets worse,
It seems there's a curse,
The slip of a pole,
Could form a big hole,
They work at incredible rate,
But it's already too late.

They look on in disgust,
Whilst covered in dust,
The place is a mess,
So full of distress,
The culprits will pay,
They caused murder today.

Rebecca Lewis (14)
Saint Martin's School For Girls

HATRED OR PEACE ENSUES

Paralysed with horror,
Frozen with disbelief.
Alone I stand
With overwhelming grief.

A weak light shines from a confused street lamp
The American flag flies defiantly,
Lives extinguished, families destroyed
New York screams but silently.

Mangled wreckage of a war-torn zone,
Billowing clouds of smoke and dust
Now enveloping this man-made tomb.
What evil exists that could do this to us?

The famous towers stand no more,
Created and destroyed by man's desire.
The memory of this merciless act
Will burn in our hearts like an endless fire.

Failing to comprehend the loss of life,
Bewildered and wondering how we all will cope.
New York is dormant, just for now,
But the heart is strong and will always have hope.

Sarah Trueman (14)
Saint Martin's School For Girls

BRAVERY

Sleep, a way of escape,
  a land far away, peaceful and calm
Sleep, a way to forget,
  to dream of a future still yet to come.

Dig down low, further and further,
  maybe some shouting will start,
Dig down low, further and further,
  ash, dust but no living things found.

One body then another,
  the count is lost,
One body then another,
  the day draws on.

Sleep, a way of escape,
  to revisit places long forgotten,
Sleep, a place for the courageous,
  where only the bravest firemen dare to go.

Jessica Banham (14)
Saint Martin's School For Girls

HORROR FROM THE SKY, SEPTEMBER 11TH

We mourn so many missing, so many dead,
Around the ruins, the grieving tread.
Those selfless servicemen and women, those at desks and
those in flight,
All powerless, overtaken by terror's might.
Many countries join in silence, in song,
Those who have seen and done no wrong.
Horror coming from the sky,
No one knows the answer, no one knows why.
Among the smouldering ashes, carnage has its place,
Now nameless threats and conflicts have a face.

Rosalind Ievins (13)
Saint Martin's School For Girls

THE FOX

Peering out of the undergrowth,
He waits for the sound of horses' hooves.
The poor fox is dirty and scruffy,
He is old and weary.

The dogs have chased him time and time again,
But every time he has managed to escape.
Yet today he may not be able to.
He sits and waits for the sound.

I hear them,
He hears them,
He runs
And so do I.

For I am an old fox too.

Holly Harbon (12)
Saint Martin's School For Girls

My Journey

My journey through life is long and hard,
I climb up many hills and mountains,
Facing new challenges every day,
But always trying to the top.

I sometimes think that I will never succeed,
Make it to the top of the high and steep mountain,
But with every doubt, fear and fall
My friends are always there to pick me up again.

The only thing worse than fear is regret,
And I have regretted many things in my journey,
But I have now learnt to laugh and smile,
Though every twist and turn in the path of life.

Noreen Kumar
Saint Martin's School For Girls

Journey

The journey through life is long and slow,
Like a metaphorical motorway through time.
Sometimes different routes may appeal to us
Yet all eventually lead back to our true selves.
With every twist and turn we may laugh or cry,
As our futures unwind.
Our dreams, our destinations forever on the horizon
As we reach what we desire,
There's a desperate want to have more, to travel further.
It's the road of life and it moves us all -
Through despair and hope,
Through weakness and strength,
'till we find our place within the queue to our end.

Sam Greenfield (15)
Saint Martin's School For Girls

CHANGING LANDSCAPES

The bleak landscape flashes by,
A mirage of dirty sand and skies.
The rocks, monumental and great,
Exquisite with their complex shapes,
Stand isolated, proud and tall,
But will they be there for evermore?

No, in time the wind and rain will cause
Those great statues to wither and fall.

The enticing waters sparkle bright,
Reflecting back the shimmering light.
How different these sights to earlier on,
But they too will, in time, be gone.

Lucy Archer (15)
Saint Martin's School For Girls

OUR JOURNEY

The experiences, which I lack,
I will learn through you.
I will warm through your eyes,
I will walk in your moments,
I will love. Like you love me.

I admire you, my love.
How little I appreciate my soulmate.
Your beauty, your wisdom.

As moments subside,
How precious you become.
My love.
Our journey together,
Our turmoils.
Your strength.

My love, my love.
How little I deserve you.
One day when I gain it all,
And lose some more.
When I cry tears of joy
And fear
And turn to you,
But you're not there.

My journey still continues,
With you by my side.
This metaphorical voyage,
Of past accounts turned true.
I lack the strength that you possess.
My God. I admire you.

Kate Pomeroy (15)
Saint Martin's School For Girls

A Journey

Tiny, yet unique,
Born innocent into the world of chaos,
So many thoughts, but no way of expressing them.
As it grows the bright blueness of its eyes disappears,
A more aware character emerges than can walk and talk,
Yet still so young in the universe of knowledge.
As school life approaches, responsibility accompanies it,
Learning about the world of wisdom.
When teenage years creep up, the face moulds yet again,
Bringing the confused and perplexed views on life.
Adulthood draws nearer and full control is taken,
A career and family are now painted in the picture.
Sounds fade and the world slows down,
The young face that once was, exists no more,
Then time stops, the wheel stops turning, and life is no more.

Katie Morton (14)
Saint Martin's School For Girls

Journey Through No-Man's-Land

Like cream covering a rich cake,
The snow crunched down where I stepped.
Dappled light fell through the trees
Not showing the secrets they kept.

The fingers of the twisting branches curled out.
Icy snow brushed across my face.
I pressed on forwards, wind whipped round my back,
As leaves danced off and left no trace.

The birds twittered at the edge of the woods.
The light ahead began to brighten.
A final glance at the mystical enchantments.
My journey was over, no longer frightened.

Rebecca Elliott (13) & Lauren Satterthwaite (12)
Saint Martin's School For Girls

The Journey Down The Giant Steps

A startling sound from down the stairs.
I climb out of my bed clutching my bears.
As I moved around the floorboards creak.
I heard the dripping of the water leak.
Down the first step I slowly go.
Was this sound friend or foe?
I wanted to go back to my cosy bed
All I wanted to do was rest my little head.
Wait a minute, where is Ted?
I know I had him when I was in bed.
Poor little Ted, his face so red.
Then a voice yells *'Back to bed!'*

Gemma Glover (12) & Francesca Williams (13)
Saint Martin's School For Girls

JOURNEYS - THE RAINBOW

The sun was shining brightly,
The rain was pouring down,
Suddenly I saw
A rainbow beyond the cloud,

I set about on foot,
To find a pot of gold,
Was I to see a leprechaun
Or was it just a fantasy?

Red, yellow, purple, blue,
Colours I could see,
As I walked towards it,
To the end of the rainbow.

Finally, I got there,
The colours started to fade,
The pot of gold had disappeared,
And nothing was to be believed.

Melissa Carter & Jaimee Le Resche (12)
Saint Martin's School For Girls

ALSATIAN

Our Alsatian barks away at night,
To keep lurking strangers out of sight!

He keeps us safe in the night and day,
He'd carry on barking if it's us one day!

He keeps us safe in the day too,
He barks and barks as if to say shoo!

We give him treats if he works hard,
Every time I look at him he is on his guard.

We wouldn't have to worry if we went away,
He will stay there every night and day.

His barking never ever ends,
But he'll still be my loveable friend!

Bianca Chambers (11)
Saint Martin's School For Girls

THE TIME OF YOUR LIFE

I embarked upon my life
Full of hope and expectations.
I was carried along
In a tidal wave
Of emotions and experiences.
My feet barely touched the ground
As I was whisked away
In the twister
Of my dreams.
All the times I had felt joy
Had been noted down, recorded and filed.
All my friends and enemies,
All the times I'd laughed. And cried.
They all flashed before my eyes.

In just those few short years,
For life is short,
Ever bumpy and winding
Never easy, straight and still,
I'd encouraged, mourned and celebrated,
Lived my life to the max.
I'd learned from experiences,
And learnt more about life and love
Than I'd ever imagined was possible
In the time of my life.

Rosalind Ievins (14)
Saint Martin's School For Girls

THE LONGEST JOURNEY EVER

One step, second step,
Stay in a straight line,
One foot, then another,
She must try to keep in time.

So many faces turn and stare,
She sees them all through a haze of white,
100 metres turn into a mile,
It is the most worrying experience of her life.

Her heart beats like a drum,
On the most magical day of her life,
It's all the emotion of the last few days,
All the pain, fun and strife.

The end is in sight,
The time has come,
To see the man,
Who her heart has won.

He turns to her,
And she dazzlingly smiles,
At last it is all over,
The journey down the aisle.

J Banham
Saint Martin's School For Girls

THE JOURNEY

The rain splashes against the window,
Lightning flashes as if there's no tomorrow.
Trees shiver in the cold,
Withering flowers beside the road.
Staring at my watch and the little hands,
Why time has stopped - I don't understand.

Kiran Branch
Saint Martin's School For Girls

THE JOURNEY

The sun beat down relentlessly,
On her thin, overworked body,
Her tired legs trembled beneath her,
As through the desert she bravely fought.

The eyes of a once strong woman,
Were cold and dark and haunting,
Her thoughts were unclear and cautious,
As she desperately sought her freedom.

Night was closing in on her now,
The dark and cold were coming,
Her strength, she felt, was failing her now,
But where would she shelter 'til morning.

The morning came as she arose,
And she continued her journey yet again,
For no time could be lost out here,
Her journey was now almost over.

Aimee Corbett (15)
Saint Martin's School For Girls

Journey

I journey to a far-off land,
Yet still within God's great hand.
I travel far away, in my dreams,
Across high hills, rivers and streams.
I trek across sun scorched deserts,
And climb up snowy mountains,
I wonder through valley and vale,
Past the water fountains.
I awake from this dream not once or twice,
Always longing still to be in paradise.
I dream to dream again,
Just to get away from life's great pain.
My pain will only go
When I meet with God,
Please let it be so.

Katrina Handford (16)
Saint Martin's School For Girls

THE BUILDING MAN BUILT

It was the building man built, colossal and tall,
And one giant blast made it crumble and fall.
It was swallowed by smoke, plummeting to the ground,
They watched in terror, they heard the sound
Of hysterical screams, crying their warning,
The whole world, then silenced, in sympathy and mourning.
The thousands lost under this terrible weight,
The biggest disaster that we have to-date.
Those without fathers, those who've lost mothers,
Trawling desolate Manhattan for brothers.
Hope they once had, but now it is dimming,
That and a huge world war may be brimming.
'New York, New York,' once famously sung,
And now when the words just roll off your tongue,
Tears well up, we stop to remember,
That fateful day - the 11th September.
The World Trade Center, the magnificent spectacle,
Where high flyers worked, smart and respectable.
Scenes now shattered, bursting the perfect bubble,
The dead and the crushed lying under its rubble.
And now all that stands is disfigured timber,
The ghostly white dust that still does linger
Over the mass graveyard, the horrendous monstrosity,
The world sending commiserations direct to the city.
The face of mankind, civilisation, tended
To shatter the moment the building imploded.

Rachel Knowles (14)
Saint Martin's School For Girls

SILENT BITE

Lurking silently in the gloom,
Dressed in black,
Armed with a hefty silenced pistol,
The spy waited.

Footsteps rang through the street,
Someone in pain,
Limped upon the glistening cobbles,
His coat billowing.

Red staining his cream trousers,
Comes from a wound,
Made by the hot lead of a concealed pistol,
His death is near.

This is to be the end,
It's unavertable,
His fingers twitched, the bullet went silently,
Biting the flesh.

The spy smiled wryly,
He slipped away,
As the victim slumped to the cold street,
His job was done . . .

Michael Horswill (13)
Solihull School

Murphy!

My fat cat . . .

Murphy's the name of my cat,
His meals are great hence him being fat,
Cos Murphy's the name of my fat cat.

He won't wander far from the house,
And the most he'll do is kill a mouse,
Cos Murphy's the name of my fat cat.

Murphy's fur is a golden ginger,
And if he wants food he'll just linger,
Cos Murphy's the name of my fat cat.

All food he loves but most of all, chicken and fish,
And never will he leave a scrap in his dish,
Cos Murphy's the name of my fat cat.

But when he is tired he lies down in his bed,
And rolls off the side, straight on top of his head,
And that's the story about Murphy,
My fat cat.

Jack Williams (13)
Solihull School

THE CIRCLE

The circle of giants gathers round,
Standing still without a sound,
For a thousand years was never found,
Stuck in the soil on top of a mound.

The petrified figures stand as still stone,
For now they are not flesh, blood and bone.
The congregation gathers round,
And they are stuck in the solid ground.

And the foolish king he stands alone,
And now is ever so famously known,
As the king who nearly conquered the land,
But was stopped by a witch's hand.

For the witch turned all eighty-one,
Into monoliths as heavy as a ton.
But the witch sacrificed herself to be,
The guardian of the circle as an Eldern tree.

But at the very dead of night,
And no one is in clear sight,
The petrified figures of stock, still stone,
Replace themselves for flesh, blood and bone.

And break from their circular link,
To go down the hill and deeply drink,
And the whispering knights start to plot,
Against the king whispering out of earshot.

But to the people they are just pieces of stone,
Standing on a hill remotely and all alone.
So the people never see them as a whole,
They don't know they have feelings or a soul.

For this army yearns for flesh, blood and bones,
But they will forever be known as the Rollright Stones.

Robert Unwin (13)
Solihull School

My Grandma

My grandma is not very smart,
She stinks of terrible socks.
And walks as slow as a snail,
Her skin is very pale.
She eats as loud as a television,
Trembles around very clumsily,
Snores when watching long videos,
And nags at me when playing consoles.
She sleeps early at nine o'clock,
Then tells me to be quiet.
She is very irritating,
Whilst I am doing my homework.
When we go to a restaurant,
She complains about the chill.
But she's going to Hong Kong at last,
I can rest in peace *finally!*

Raymond Cheung (13)
Solihull School

Poem About My Brother

My brother doesn't wash his face,
His hair is never trim.
My brother's not afraid of germs,
But they're afraid of him.

My brother is a boy of ten,
But he acts more like three,
It's really is a shame
That when he makes a mess,
Guess who gets all the blame!

My brother has cookery classes after school,
But his food is rather cruel
And I think we should leave his pasties to the mules.

He walks like a donkey,
But he acts more like a monkey,
As he walks down the streets itching his hair,
I begin to think he looks more like a bear.

Rikesh Chauhan (13)
Solihull School

A Little Old Lady

In my family she's the oldest member
She lives alone in her home with no one to talk to
Her skin, crinkly and her face is like the glowing ember
She's very lonely and needs to speak to you
The clothes she wears are crumpled and musty
The only thing that keeps her company is the clock that goes 'Cuckoo'
And her old, but clean hair is as white as a husky
This little old lady is very brave, she's been through it all
The wars and her husband dying
She's sad and alone without a friend
We tell her everything that's happened - what's the point in lying?
So could anyone please be so kind to lend
This little old lady a friend?

Sam Jackson (13)
Solihull School

SPYING ON A COLD, WINDY WINTER NIGHT

The frosty air stung his throat
As he made for a man in a brown coat
Then moving like a crafty fox
He crept slowly up the creaky docks
As quick as a flash
Into the shadows he did pass
His gaunt face and worried eyes
Looked out from the shadows where he lies.

Then from the shadows he did see
The other bend down and place something on the quay
He didn't move until the other had completely departed
And slowly, ever so slowly, he started
To walk to the spot under which the plan hid
When he found it he pulled off the lid
So with the plan into the darkness he took flight
On that cold, windy winter night.

Stewart Hunter (12)
Solihull School

KIT'S WILDERNESS

Useless all alone,
No life in my home,
No friends to believe,
Nightmares at night's eve.

Games of death and luck,
Pictures made of muck,
In this cave of death,
No time to breathe a breath,
Tension here and there,
Play this if you dare.
I have nothing to concede,
The 'death game' must be my deed.

David Diez-Jones (13)
Solihull School

My Grandad

My grandad is up at 5.45,
Gathering the cup, the milk and the tea,
Ready to make himself a fresh pot of tea.
Making no noise as he trundles downstairs,
Waking nobody because he cares.
As he finally makes it to the lounge,
He creeps to a seat and manages to sit down.

He reads his book, like a wise old owl,
Studying every word, without a sound to be heard.
Then up to the post office, to get his paper and post the mail,
He takes his time, like a slow moving snail.

He sleeps, on and off, in his chair all day.
Dreaming his life away.
Then he shakes himself wide awake,
The highlight of the day is on next,
It's 4.30, the time has come,
Countdown has begun.

James Lishman (13)
Solihull School

The Traitor

Silent as a mouse and as large as life,
Parker hid in shadows armed with gun and knife.
Message in his hand, he started to run,
He was a spy and this was no pun.

He entered the park and sat down on the bench,
The message he was holding was written in French.
His hawk like eyes swung left and right,
Until he saw a silhouette against the dark night.

He shuffled on the bench and lifted his finger,
The dark silhouette, it began to linger
Towards the park bench where Parker sat,
Sat down next to him and took off his hat.

Into this hat a message Parker put,
Then the other stabbed him right above the foot.
The traitor that had killed him, left the park at nine,
The stars were the only ones that saw his crime.

Matthew Ralph (12)
Solihull School

THE SECRET AGENT

T he spy tiptoed behind the tree,
H e despised the ugly scar on his knee,
E ven now he wanted revenge on the man hiding beyond
 the cold Stonehenge.

S till he keeps his anger low,
E very step he takes is slow,
C reeping along the cobbled street,
R evising the plan, who will he meet,
E yebrows singed and fairly black,
T he spy then heard a chilling thwack.

A gent Jones ran to the scene,
G ot to a place where he had never been,
E verywhere the screams rang out,
N asty words were echoing about,
T here in the street lay the mission incomplete without dismission.

Richard Jerrom (12)
Solihull School

BORING ENGLISH LESSON

I charged through the streets, silent as the night,
A man popped out, it gave me quite a fright,
I'd never seen him, but asked for a fight,
I hit him with a left and then with a right,
And then I ran on as silent as the night.

My followers were after me, for that I was sure,
I saw a very old house, and knocked hard on its door,
A bald man opened it; he looked about fifty-four,
He stood firm on a magnificent, candlelit floor,
He couldn't fool me; he was an enemy for sure!

I had to go fast, there was not much time,
I looked at my watch; it was half past nine,
I ran into the show it cost me a dime,
I ran onto the stage, into the bright light shine,
I ran up the black steps, I was *just* on time.

I couldn't see very well, so I pulled out my sword,
My master came up to me, I said, 'Hello Lord.'
'You have done very well boy,' and he gave me an award,
The organ started to play, it struck out on a chord,
'It's scary what I can do when I am really bored!'

Paul Griffin (12)
Solihull School

The Agent

The agent lurks in the dark of the night,
He slips through shadows with all his might,
As cunning as a fox,
He hid in a box.

The agent sits there on a stool,
Drinking beer, acting cool,
He attempts to stifle enemy plans,
By discovering codes hidden in cans.

There's nothing you can do to save your fate,
The agent's coming, it's too late,
You may as well be already dead,
For he will shoot you in the head.

A man popped out of the darkened night,
I saw his face and asked for a fight,
I hit him with a left and then a right,
My enemy gone I left the site.

Peter Calvert (13)
Solihull School

THE STUPID AGENT

He slipped through shadows like a cat,
A sly as a rat,
He wore corduroy trousers,
And a silk scarlet hat.

He was poised like a snake,
And he tried to pounce on the prey,
But he trod on a rake,
And it gave him away.

The man turned around,
And away he did bound,
As the clumsy agent drew his pistol,
And shot him through the ear hole.

His mission was a failure,
As the man should be alive,
But he couldn't let him get away,
So now he will die.

Tom Harrison (12)
Solihull School

SWIFT AND SILENT

He was wearing a smart black suit,
He prowled through the shadows,
He was as quiet as a leaf,
But he knew his purpose.

His unsuspecting prey was near,
He moved in for the kill,
Quickly he readied his pistol,
And silently took aim.

He stood like an attacking hawk,
His target like a vole,
The man was an enemy spy,
So he squeezed the trigger.

The swift bullet zoomed through the air,
And tore through the man's head.
The spy returned to the shadows,
Leaving the corpse behind.

Sean Maguire (12)
Solihull School

MALICE MAN

A man full of malice and disguise
Watching with taunting, eerie, dark eyes
Unseen, but there, his presence is unknown
He works a web until his cover is blown.

He enters buildings, conferences, groups
Without notice he sneaks, informs and snoops
His job is to find out whatever he can
To undermine oppositions' major plan.

No mention of failure can be found in his mind
A trail of demolition is left behind
All he does is enter a pact
Until the time comes to start his act.

But when he has finished his secretive arts
He quickly flies like the wind and departs
To go to his next undercover mission or job
Of ideas the enemy again he will rob.

Duncan Brown (12)
Solihull School

THE SECRET AGENT

He sweeps through the shadowed alleys,
Chased by some weird mad men,
As stealthy as an owl,
Running for his country and his life,
Holding the information to the world,
Guarding it with his life,
His life is so vital,
His mission so dangerous.

The enemy has him surrounded,
Like a bird in a cage,
Squawking for lots of help,
Closing in like a pack of grey wolves,
The prey is running like a cheetah,
The predator is near,
But the prey is so sly,
And escapes without a scratch, unharmed!

Oliver Talbot (12)
Solihull School

SPYING

As she walked along the street,
Keeping a sense of normality,
Her black coat trailing behind her,
Her identity still unclear to me,
She leapt into the shadows,
Like a cheetah she pounced so quickly,
I quickly shuffled after her,
I was left alone, there was only me.

But then my eyes fell upon,
A piece of parchment on the floor,
And inscribed on it was a note,
It said, 'Stay away from my Eleanor.'
Puzzled by this strange statement,
I found a footprint on the floor,
Which I followed fearlessly,
To a large oak bolted door.

I knocked down the strong oak door,
To find inside a small, pale room,
And in a cot I found a child,
Even the child had a face of gloom,
And on the dresser beside the cot,
I found another note which said,
'My darling Eleanor, goodbye.'
A woman lay shot in the head.

Nicholas Lunn (12)
Solihull School

Mission - Possible

The chopper blades cut through the air,
And the wind blew through the agent's hair.
The agent dropped from the chopper,
The evil mistress, he was going to stop her.

As he crept down the stair,
He knew he was close to the mistress's lair.
Into the laboratory, he did sneak,
To find the bomb, and take a peek.

When he knew he couldn't stop the timer,
He knew his chances were getting finer.
Then the mistress came round the corner,
He knew the mistress was much stronger.

He pulled out his gun and shot some lead,
And then he hit her, square in the head.
He got out just in time,
So he knew that he was fine.

Rob Henderson (13)
Solihull School

A Spy's Tail

The most wanted man of time,
Bigger than bulky and thicker than slime,
Hunted by the sleek and shot by the blind,
The most wanted man of time.

The fastest guy in all the country,
Hunts for food and hunts for bounty,
Strong as a bull and quick as a bunny,
The fastest guy in all the country.

The most wanted man of time,
Runs quicker than water through grime,
The fastest guy in all the country,
Charges like a bull and hunts like a bunny.

The fastest guy in all the country,
Pounces like a cat and floors its bounty,
The most wanted man of time turned to poultry,
By the fastest spy in all the country.

Anthony Allso (12)
Solihull School

THE PERFECT SPY

A spy should be silent
Like a panther on the prowl.
A spy should be stealthy
Like a fox hunting fowl.

A spy should be powerful
Like an ox pulling a plough.
A spy should be camouflaged
Like a lizard on a bough.

A spy should have vision
Like the eyes of a hawk.
A spy should be confident
And deceptive in his talk.

A spy should be skilful
Like a blacksmith at work.
A spy should be aware
For dangers that may lurk.

James Bond and his mates
May be over the hill,
But like all perfect spies
They had a . . .

License to kill!

David Mundy (12)
Solihull School

THE SECRET AGENT

The long mackintosh he once wore,
Floated on the top of the Severn Bare.
For he had thrown it with all his might,
Into the sooty, black night.

Now he pondered through the dark streets,
Hoping to find his neat little motor,
In a corner of a cobbled lot,
And drive away, far away.

Inserted the key and pressed the pedal,
Listening to the quiet, churning engine.
Peeling off his clothes, damp with blood,
Smelling the awful stench of the mud.

Chucking them out of an opened window,
Hoping for the stealth of the sodden things,
So - no one would find them,
And find out the awful crime he had committed.

Brandon Cooney (12)
Solihull School

MY MUM

My mum,
    She's always bright and cheery.
My mum,
    She's sometimes very eerie.

My mum,
    She smells very nice.
My mum,
    She's also full of spice.

My mum,
    She dresses like a flower.
My mum,
    She never acts sour.

My mum,
    She is very swift.
My mum,
    She is the very best gift in the world.

Timothy Freeman (13)
Solihull School

THE ELEDUCKBAT

The Eleduckbat is a wonderfig thing,
With a hose for a nose and tusks on its wing.
It hangs downsideup like a featherous balloon,
And trumbles along neath a melonymoon.

The Eleduckbat is a heaftig beast,
Quackabuns make its favoursome feast.
It swims with webbed tootsies in puddlyooze,
And turns bottoms up for its afternogg snooze.

When happig its voice is shrillasonic,
But when it is thummerous its trumpet is chronic.
Its eggs are squound with a leatherig shell,
Don't wandig too close - there's a pongery smell!

Christopher Troth (11)
Solihull School

Lurking In The Shadows...

In and out of the shadows,
Merging with the crowd,
Lurking in the alleyways,
Inconspicuous on the street.

Long, flowing, great coat,
Hiding behind his hat,
Scarf wrapped up around his neck,
Hands stuffed deep in baggy pockets.

Ever wandering darting eyes,
The ubiquitous moustache,
Beard and glasses obscure the face,
Bushy eyebrows complete the disguise.

Contact made, message despatched,
His mission now complete,
The information is safe and sound,
Into the shadows back he goes.

Alistair Higgins (12)
Solihull School

THE SECRET AGENT

The agent is an elusive man
He always has a master plan
In the darkness of the shadows he lurks
He never gives up his lifetime work

You'll never see him in the street
You'll never see him on the beat
You'll never ever give him a scare
You'll never catch him unaware

The cunning of a fox hunting prey
He finds shadows even on the brightest day
Everybody would love to have his head
Many terrorists want him dead

But they all fail in their fiendish plot
He overpowers them more often than not
It's not that easy to kill this man
I don't think anybody can

He's as wise as an owl and as fast as a cheetah
He doesn't have a wife and he doesn't want one either
He lurks around alleys and trash
He makes midnight raids what a dash

He pounces on you before you can think
He can kill you with just a wink
His fists are lethal and dangerous
His luxury suites are very spacious

You'll find him ever so incredulous
But when you're rescued you will be gracious
He's like a small scurrying rat
He knows to avoid deadly traps

Somehow he always comes through
To win the day for me and you
To save the world from destruction
And to blow away evil obstructions.

Philip Achille (12)
Solihull School

LURKING

In the black, heartless night they lurk
Behind dark pillars and on dark benches
Beneath large bowler hats they smirk
People lower their hard defences.

They cover people like a large hawk
With knives and guns and great senses
Beneath the gutters, leaders they stalk
Like foxes they smite the chickens' defences.

They offer their lives as forfeit
Then steal secrets for others' profit
Unseen with malevolent speed
He has committed the foul deed.

These spies are secret enemies
Like shadows in the black, starry night
They eat their prey like sea anemones
It takes great times indeed to make these spies fight.

Steven Bryce (13)
Solihull School